After the

Quality Audit

Also available from ASQ Quality Press

The Quality Audit Handbook
ASQ Quality Audit Division, J. P. Russell, editing director

Quality Audits for Improved Performance, Second Edition
Dennis R. Arter

Internal Quality Auditing
Denis Pronovost

Meet the Registrar: Firsthand Accounts of ISO 9000 Success from the Registration Source
C. Michael Taylor

Fundamentals of Quality Auditing
B. Scott Parsowith

Quality Management Benchmark Assessment, Second Edition
J.P. Russell

The Quality Audit: A Management Evaluation Tool
Charles A. Mills

Puzzling Auditing Puzzles
J. P. Russell and Janice Russell

Root Cause Analysis: Simplified Tools and Techniques
Bjørn Andersen and Tom Fagerhaug

To request a complimentary catalog of ASQ Quality Press publications, call 800-248-1946, or visit our online bookstore at http://qualitypress.asq.org .

AFTER THE
QUALITY AUDIT

Closing the Loop on the Audit Process

Second Edition

J. P. Russell
Terry Regel

ASQ Quality Press
Milwaukee, Wisconsin

Library of Congress Cataloging-in-Publication Data

Russell, J. P. (James P.), 1945–
    After the quality audit : closing the loop on the audit process / J.P. RTussell, Terry
Regel.—2nd ed.
        p.   cm.
Includes bibliographical references and index.
ISBN 0-87389-486-3
    1. Management audit.   2. Quality control—Auditing.   3. Quality assurance.   I. Regel,
Terry, 1950-   II. Title.

HD58.95 .R87 2000
658.5'62—dc21   00-026672

© 2000 by ASQ

10 9 8 7 6 5 4 3 2

ISBN 0-87389-486-3

Acquisitions Editor: Ken Zielske
Project Editor: Annemieke Koudstaal
Production Administrator: Shawn Dohogne
Special Marketing Representative: Matthew Meinholz

ASQ Mission: The American Society for Quality advances individual and organizational
performance excellence worldwide by providing opportunities for learning, quality improvement,
and knowledge exchange.

Attention: Bookstores, Wholesalers, Schools and Corporations: ASQ Quality Press books,
videotapes, audiotapes, and software are available at quantity discounts with bulk purchases for
business, educational, or instructional use. For information, please contact ASQ Quality Press at
800-248-1946, or write to ASQ Quality Press, P.O. Box 3005, Milwaukee, WI 53201-3005.

To place orders or to request a free copy of the ASQ Quality Press Publications Catalog, including
ASQ membership information, call 800-248-1946. Visit our web site at www.asq.org. or
http://qualitypress.asq.org.

Printed in the United States of America

  Printed on acid-free paper

American Society for Quality

Quality Press
600 N. Plankinton Avenue
Milwaukee, Wisconsin 53203
Call toll free 800-248-1946
www.asq.org
http://qualitypress.asq.org
http://standardsgroup.asq.org

It is impossible to solve significant problems using the same knowledge that created them.

—*Albert Einstein*

Contents

Preface

The power behind eliminating problems is yet to be realized. We are concerned that there are so many auditors finding problems and too few of the problems being eliminated that it was necessary to write this book.

If organizations want to optimize the use of their resources, auditors and those being audited need to work as a team, on equal ground. There has been a ground swell, as people come to realize: Why do audits if we don't benefit from them?

The new century brings with it organizations that are fine tuning their management techniques for optimal use of resources and changes to the ISO 9001 quality management standard that promotes flexibility and achievement of customer satisfaction.

The full potential behind eliminating problems found during audits has yet to be realized. We are concerned that too few of the problems being found are being eliminated. If organizations want to optimize the use of their resources, auditors and those being audited must work as a team, with the same goals and on equal ground.

After four years of consulting and presenting the After the Quality Audit class for ASQ, we thought it was time to update the text and share some of the things that we have learned.

The second edition is almost 20% larger and features:

- A new chapter devoted to the Reason-Pain Matrix (R-P). The Reason-Pain Matrix **links audit findings and program results to business** objectives.

- Four new appendices to highlight **practical experience and ideas for improving** the report and follow-up process.
- Sidebars throughout the text with **lessons learned.**
- Modifications to align with the **new ISO 9000 series.**
- Better flow and presentation of material

The most important part is the addition of many new topics to address contemporary issues. Some of the topics are:

- top seven reasons for ineffective corrective action from practitioners,
- use of system actuators for making system changes,
- model for writing a finding statement,
- how to assess the audit program effectiveness,
- six simple analytical tools to be used in every audit report,
- noncomformity statement strengths and weaknesses,
- approaches for handling chronic unresponsiveness to corrective action requests,
- figuring the cost of a customer complaint,
- ideas for auditing surveys,
- ideas for improving the report,
- ideas for effective follow-up and audit program management,
- changing personal behavior to make compliance audits better,
- a new business system model, and
- overcoming redundant audits.

As your quality system matures, we believe this book and its future editions, is an absolute must.

Acknowledgments

We have received many comments and success stories from so many people we can only acknowledge their general contribution to this second edition. Working with J. P. to translate their input into text has been an enjoyable learning experience. I must also thank my wife, Pat, who contributed to the completion of this edition through her reviews of text revisions and editorial experience.

Terry

I am pleased to be able to write the second edition. I would like to acknowledge Terry Regel for prodding, pushing, hinting, and showing up at my office in July 1999 to kick-off the second edition. Though I have many interests, this work is particularly important and has helped organizations improve. I would like to acknowledge the dozens of quality professionals who encouraged us with their success stories.

J. P.

Introduction

The past few years have brought a proliferation of ISO 9000-based quality systems. Correspondingly, the number of consultants and auditors available to help organizations prepare for ISO registration has increased. We have noticed in our work that no matter how good the consultant or the client organization, there is a recurring pattern. The same problems are found, reported, and corrected in one audit after another, but they still continue to occur. After reviewing many occurrences of this phenomenon, we came to realize that the solution lies between the performance of the audit and the follow-up audit. In other words, somewhere between the delivery of the auditor's product (the audit report) and the customer's use of the product (corrective action) there is a breakdown. As quality professionals and auditors, this concerns us because we know that this is not the way the process should work.

This book is not about the audit process. There are already many good books on quality auditing that discuss the preparation, performance, reporting, and closure of audits, but most of these leave the reader with the impression that follow-up audits are the rule rather than the exception. The reality is that many clients view the audit report as the end of the audit and the end of the auditor's involvement in the process. In other words, only three-fourths of the process is being completed. As a result, customers are not getting the benefits of the audit process.

Neither is this book written just for auditors. It is written for general management, supervisors, audit program managers, auditors, examiners, and anyone who seeks improvement from audits. To succeed (get benefits), all the players in the improvement process (auditors, auditees, general management, supervisors, audit managers) must work together as a team rather than being at odds with each other.

Contrary to popular belief, the purpose of an audit is not just to identify those things that are wrong. We have found time and again that the auditee already knows that not only are "things" wrong, but also knows which "things" are wrong. However, the auditee (all too frequently) cannot identify the system failures. The purpose of an audit, then, is to identify the system failures so that the auditee may initiate appropriate corrective/preventive actions. Appropriate corrective/preventive actions change the process or system so that the problems are fixed for good.

Before we started to work on this book, we found that the fundamental problem with most audit programs is not with auditor techniques during the audit. The problem is the auditee's failure to benefit from the audit process through corrective action. We also identified several reasons for this:

- The "problem" is not investigated thoroughly by the auditors.
- The "problem" is not communicated effectively to the auditee.
- The corrective action process is not understood by the auditee.
- The corrective action process does not address the root cause.
- The auditee does not understand the auditor's role in this process.

With that in mind, this book does not address the initial stages of the audit process. The portion of the audit that is of primary concern in this book is after the performance of the audit (i.e., from audit report preparation through the corrective action process). The focus of the book is as follows:

- Finding problems,
- Making sure the problem is understood,
- Acknowledging the interrelationships between problem finders and problem solvers,
- Ensuring the solutions work, and
- Ensuring the audit program is managed effectively.

Auditing, with its various aliases (assessment, evaluation, etc.), has become popular in the 1990s. The audit process is responsible for identifying problems that organizations often "sweep under the rug." Hiding problems, which has been our MO (modus operandi), is not good for business and certainly does not promote continuous quality improvement.

We will address continuous quality improvement only to a limited degree. While we recognize its importance, it is outside the scope of this book. Of the "three quality improvement camps" identified by Jim Van Patton of Trinity Performance Systems, we will, for the most part, limit our discussion to solving problems identified in audits (assessments, evaluations, etc.).

A dependable process to ensure that we find the underlying causes of a problem and then determine a long-term solution for that problem has been evading us. This situation should not surprise us, since we are inundated with poor examples of problem resolutions within organizations and society. Many organizations seem to have the time to do things over, but not enough time to fix them correctly. Furthermore, there is a media frenzy to point out problems and ensure that the guilty are punished, but rarely do we hear about how the system was changed to prevent recurrence of problems. We must conclude that the media has decided that the long-term solutions are not newsworthy. For example, most of us know about the Hubble Telescope problem and that it was repaired, but few know about the efforts to change design and production systems to ensure that a similar problem does not occur with future projects.

Another major concern preventing the resolution of problems is that many managers feel the same way about quality system auditors as you may feel about IRS auditors. An observer might easily identify your lack of trust through your change of posture and the tightening around your eyes as you hear the words, "Hello, I am from the IRS. I am here to help you." In the same way, most managers cannot accept that an auditor truly has come to help. The sad part about this situation is that we, the auditors, have done little to dispel their fears.

One of the goals of this book is to provide techniques for improving the relationship between auditors, auditees, and management while improving the corrective action process. In order to achieve this goal, we have developed the Audit Function Improvement Process. Of course, we also discuss effective audit reports, presenting the audit results, and the problem-solving process before we introduce the Audit Function Improvement Process.

This book progresses through the following steps:

- Understanding the meaning of corrective and preventive action—we need to be able to see the big picture and understand the lingo.

- Discussing the relationship of audit input to the corrective action process and how to provide effective inputs to corrective action—if we start with garbage we will end up with garbage.

- Understanding the principles of the corrective/preventive action process—we cannot do it unless we know what it is we should be doing.

- Presenting and discussing the Audit Function Improvement Process—step-by-step activities and examples.

- Discussing methods for ensuring that organizations are maximizing the benefits of the corrective action process—why do it if we don't benefit?

- Evaluating audit program management and providing methods for improving effectiveness—poor audit program management may be the major roadblock to improvement.

- Closing the loop by discussing other potential causes of ineffective corrective action from audit investigations using cause-and-effect analysis—leaving no stone unturned until we uncover all causes of ineffectiveness.

We provide many examples throughout the book, and we "call them like we see them." It is not our intention to offend any individual, group, or organization. This book serves as a reality check to see if you are serious about reaping the benefits of the audit process or are just going through the motions in order to get credit for conducting the audits or checking off the audit results.

An organization's audit program should result in improved performance. If your organization is like many, you have trained auditors. But 90 percent of the training was in the interpretation of performance standards (ISO 9000, the Malcolm Baldrige National Quality Award criteria, etc.) and how to detect failures. This book describes closing the loop on the audit process and the relationship between auditors, stakeholders, and management for getting results that benefit (not hinder) the organization. After all, that is what the audit process is all about. Isn't it?

Chapter 1

Reporting Problems

How Did We Get Here?

Hundreds of thousands of auditors are finding hundreds of millions of problems, but few organizations are really fixing what was found. Organizations are spending significant resources on auditing and are wondering where the payback is. Management is asking; "How is this helping? What are the benefits?" The answer is that there will be very few benefits unless organizations start closing the loop on the audit process.

Teams of auditors and examiners look under every rock and in every nook and cranny to find problems that need to be fixed and opportunities for improvement. There are internal organization auditors, customer auditors, independent registrar auditors, auditors to check auditors, and government auditors. They are checking products, services, processes, and systems. We have seen literally volumes of tabulated problems stored in books, three-ring binders, and spreadsheets as a type of testimonial to the efforts and work of all the auditors, assessors, and examiners. The difficulty with these problem lists is that organizations are doing a lousy job of getting any benefit from this massive effort to find what they are doing wrong. In short, organizations are doing a great job pointing out the problems, but a poor job of deciding which are important and then fixing the problems so that they do not happen again.

What about your organization? Are you constantly advancing, or are you taking one step backward for every two steps forward? Many organizations are taking as many steps backward as forward, or worse, losing ground. One common step backward comes from wasting internal resources due to poorly managed corrective action, evaluation, and follow-up programs.

You may be using auditing, customer surveys, and employee suggestion systems to identify problems or opportunities within your organization, business, or process. You may be assessing your system compared to international quality management standards. Your organization may be assessed against quality award criteria, environmental management, or for safety. Most organizations, however, are not getting the benefits that they should from their corrective/preventive actions programs.

The primary focus of this book is how to get the desired improvement from audits, from the identification of problems through their resolution. Our pledge is to stay true to this focus, so we will not be able to accommodate every term to fit every nuance of the improvement process. We will, however, define and clarify terms that we use so that we all have a common understanding as we travel along the corrective/preventive action process road together.

Value Added or Non–Value Added?

All processes must have a starting point (the input) and an end point (the output). For the corrective/preventive action process, the starting point is the identification of a problem, situation, concern, defect, nonconformance, finding, observation, or noncompliance. For convenience, we will use the word problem in this book.

Every problem has a pain factor, or it would not be a problem. The *pain* means the consequences to the organization, manager, or individual for not fixing the problem. The pain (consequences) may be so serious that something must be done right now, or the pain may be minor (of little consequence) and you can live with it (it's no big deal, it's really more of an inconvenience). Insignificant pains may be isolated (the crick in your neck this morning) and so are not really a problem—they will go away—or they are so minor that it is not worth spending any time worrying about it. Let's say you noticed when dining out that the waiter served your drink on your left side (proper etiquette is that drinks are served on the right). Do you inform the waiter of the error, report it to management, and demand that management issue a corrective action plan with a training program and competence tests? Or do you continue the conversation with your friends and enjoy your beverage? Obviously, some problems are more important than others.

In the organizational world, many times problems (opportunities) are listed in some type of report as a result of a quality audit, examination, self-assessment, and/or brainstorming of work groups. The most significant increase in problem identification is coming from the establishment of audit (assessment) programs as required by the ISO 9001 requirement standard (specifically the internal audit clause 8.2) and from the Malcolm Baldrige National Quality Award examinations. The audit process may end with reporting the problem (output). International audit standards state that the audit is completed upon submission of the audit report to the client.[1] However, the problem statement is just the beginning (the input) of the corrective/preventive action process. Problem reporting is fast becoming the focal point for improvement within organizations. The correction of problems is consuming vast resources within organizations, as it is human nature to want to put problems behind us. A simple process for finding and fixing problems is depicted in Figure 1.1.

Many audit reports are problem lists and, as such, are poor excuses for a management report. If you are interested in improvement, audit and assessment reports that are of the laundry-list variety should not be accepted by management. Exceptions to this rule are audit reports being used as an implementation tool for a quality system or plan and audits conducted for the sole purpose of compliance verification. A problem listing report may consist of: (1) facts found or observed events, (2) nonconformance statements, or (3) a subjective list of what an auditor thinks might be wrong. It is common for the reports to be a singular or mixed list of

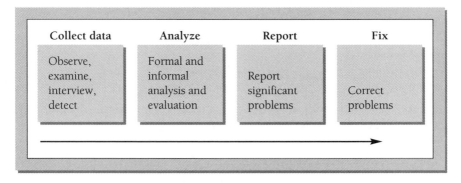

Figure 1.1. Finding and fixing problems: simplified process.

nonconformities, defects, noncompliances, observations, concerns, etc. But even worse are the reports that are subjective opinion rather than fact.

Lists of problems that do not take into account their relative importance, do not reference standards or company objectives not being fulfilled, or do not support judgments with facts are worthless. They are worthless as a tool for improvement or for changing the way we do business. These indifferent lists are consuming scarce organizational resources and the organization is getting almost no benefit from their auditing efforts. Compare the following statements.

Non–Value-Added List (not useful):

1. There were damaged product packages in the warehouse.

2. There was no revision level on the audit procedure.

3. Rental units (facilities, material, equipment) were not clean.

Value-Added List (analyzed, studied):

1. There were three damaged product packages in the warehouse (lot number xxx1-12, xx10-44 and xxx33-2). Product package lot xx10 was in the prep area ready for shipment. Review of customer complaints showed that 28 percent of all customer distribution complaints are due to damaged packaging.

2. Three different people had three different versions of the audit procedure. Since the procedure changes include format changes and word definition changes, managers are not sure how to respond to audit reports. The Ag department is currently waiting for clarification of the last audit report. The lack of version control may be causing delays in corrective action initiatives.

3. Three (3) of ten (10) rental units ready for customer use were not cleaned per SOP. There is no control system (audit, inspection, checklist sign-off, etc.) to verify that units are being cleaned per SOP, nor is there any method for customer feedback regarding unclean units (not on customer evaluation form).

The non–value-added list will result in corrective action such as the following:

Corrective Action for #1: Damaged product packages were removed from storage and sent to the repackaging department.

Corrective Action for #2: Audit procedure was reissued with a revision level indicated.

Corrective Action for #3: Instructed the second shift to be more careful.

The customer of the audit doesn't know by reading the report whether the problem is an isolated incident or represents a system problem. In the non–value-added list, Number 1 may only represent two damaged product packages, yet the report states that product packaging is damaged. It may be the only one out of a thousand, but the reader of the report doesn't know that. Consequently, the report will either be regarded as nit-picking (looking for imperfection) and of little value, or resources may be marshaled to solve a problem that doesn't exist.

The non–value-added list does not lead to change or improvement of system problems. There is no motivation (the pain has not been identified) to change the system or process. The value-added list is a step forward, but is still just a list. Facts are used in the value-added list to support why these problems may be important to management (the evaluated organization).

Systems Thinking

In the previous paragraph we used the phrase *system problems*, yet we have found that most people have difficulty understanding and describing what a system is. For example, you might have heard the saying: "Once is an incidence; twice is a coincidence; three times is a system," or that "people develop systematic ways of doing things." They might illustrate what they mean in the following manner:

> People normally arrive at work at a certain time every weekday, some have a system to arrive 30 minutes early, while some people normally arrive just before or just after the whistle (and have an excuse ready). Even apparently unorganized people have a system, they just don't realize it.

What is actually being described is a process, not a system. What is being described is the collection of activities required for a person to arrive at work on time. By our definition, a process *is a collection of activities with a single result or output.* A system *is a collection of processes supported by an infrastructure to manage and coordinate its function,* such as a management system in an organization.

To effectively address problems, you should think in terms of processes and systems. For example, if it takes 30 minutes to get to work and one hour to get ready, setting the alarm clock one hour before starting time will never get you to work on time. To get to work on time you need to change the process. Trying harder or wishing is not going to cut it, you must change the process. We do not know the solution for you. It may be to set the alarm clock 30 minutes earlier, or it may be not to soak in the tub for 40 minutes every day. You, the stakeholder of the process, must investigate the situation and come up with a process that is capable: capable of getting you to work on time, every day.

Systems thinking is evaluating a single process in its relationship to the related processes and defining the cause(s) of the problem. An excellent tool to use is the cause-and-effect diagram because it helps "filter" the process interrelationships to identify the root cause. If you don't address the cause(s), the process will not change—there will be no improvement—and the problem will recur.

If you disagree, stop and think about the number of times you have heard, or said, "I know what's wrong. I've fixed that problem at least a half dozen times." The truth is that if you had "fixed it" the first time you would not have had to fix it all those other times. What you did was employ the maxim, "If I don't have time to do it over, I am never going to have time to do it right." The problem with the quick fix, or remedial (containment) action, is that it only alleviates the symptoms—it does not correct the cause. So, we will have the opportunity to "fix it" over and over again. If you employ systems thinking, you will look beyond the symptoms to the related processes and systems and trace the problem back to its source of origin.

When you compare the resources to resolve problems in this manner versus the "quick fix," you will find the results quite surprising. For example, by addressing their delays in monthly closing as a systems issue, rather than a myriad of symptoms, one company was able to reduce their month-end accounting activities from a 15-day ordeal to 4 days, which they have maintained for two years. (This accomplishment is a new benchmark for their family of companies.)

The dividing line between a system and a process can be elusive. One way to illustrate the difference is to think of all the comforts in the structure of a house as a system; the underlying features of the rooms as the processes that provide those comforts would also make up a system. The system is transparent: you normally don't see it, unless you get out the wrecking bar to pull away wall board or shingles to reveal such things as electrical wiring, hot water pipes, junction boxes, studs, and air conditioner vents. If the house is part of a farm with a barn, silo, chicken house, and pasture, the house could be considered a subsystem of the farm.

Organizations are comprised of processes, as shown in Figure 1.2. Each process can be defined by evaluating people, equipment, materials, measures, methods, and environmental inputs and outputs. The

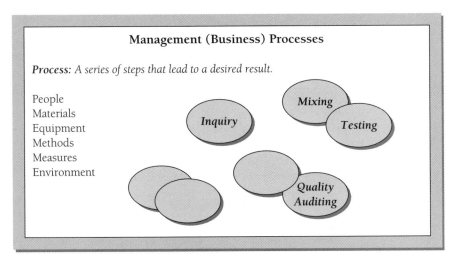

Figure 1.2.   Management (business) processes.

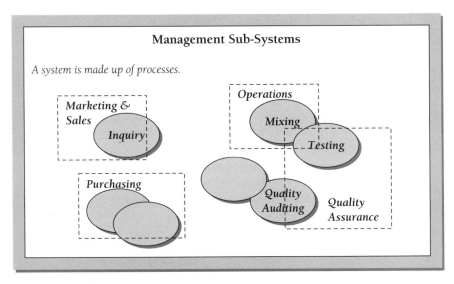

Figure 1.3.   Management sub-systems.

processes may be grouped to form subsystems for a larger organization, as shown in Figure 1.3.

Organizations may have a system for purchasing, production, operations, research, engineering, marketing, and so on. When you add customers and put the systems together with input and outputs, you have a

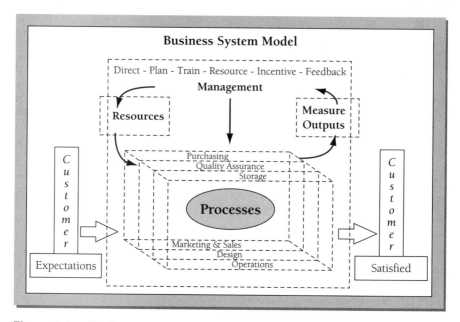

Figure 1.4. Business system model.

dynamic business system (see Figure 1.4). The input starts with customer requirements (market need). The organization plans, secures resources, and provides the product or service to meet the need. The system output is data and the value-added product or service for customer satisfaction. The information from the processes and customer satisfaction is analyzed and used by management for improving the system to better meet the customer needs. When you combine businesses (such as in a big corporation), you have a conglomerated system.

A system is composed of processes (accepting orders, forming, cleaning, molding, replacing, issuing, testing) that some define as the "-ing" words (but the "-ing" rule is not always the case). The linking of two or more processes creates a system. The system is formed to provide focus and an environment for the processes. Let us assume that management creates the system and that the system is created to influence the behavior of people so that management is able to achieve certain goals and objectives. We propose that management uses the following *system actuators* to influence behavior (see Figure 1.4):

1. Directives (orders, policy, mission, and procedures)

2. Planning (setting targets and goals)

3. Training (classroom, video, or by example)
4. Resources (technology, equipment, people, monetary wealth, or fixed assets)
5. Incentives (both positive and negative, rewards and punishment)
6. Feedback (feeding information back, such as measures to constantly adjust the processes to achieve the desired outputs)

Management normally uses a combination of these system affectors to implement changes. The tools used to influence behavior may be considered processes (such as the training process or planning process), which is okay, but it is the combination of them that creates the overall environment for meeting organizational objectives. More details will follow in chapter 7 when we discuss the audit program management system.

Auditors evaluate and analyze the system(s) and individual processes to report conclusions about the effectiveness of the management system. While we may identify a "problem" within a process, it is the system that holds the key to its solution.

Purposeful and Focused Reporting

The purpose of the audit is stated in several standards and guidelines, but what is the purpose of the audit report? What will the report be used for? Who are the customers of the audit report?

The purpose of the quality *audit report* is to communicate the results of an investigation. The report should provide correct and clear data that will be effective as a management aid in addressing important organizational issues. Reports should identify systematic errors (important problems), not de-rail management efforts by finding imperfection and identifying minor isolated errors. *System error* is something that is repeated or has a pattern, something inherent in the way business is conducted. Isolated errors are nonrepeating, where no pattern can be established. Most of the time, isolated errors either point out human imperfection or are symptoms of a bigger system or process problem.

Effective Report Guidelines

Report the Right Fact. Making a list of nonconformities, facts, deficiencies, etc., is the simplest method of reporting the results of an evaluation. The auditor only finds and reports what is found. During one audit, an auditor found that there was a discrepancy between the equipment master list and the calibration log. The master list indicated that a certain piece of equipment had been taken out of service, but the calibration log indicated continued calibration at the appropriate interval. The auditor could accurately report a nonconformity for not maintaining calibration records, yet it would be incorrect because the fault was not with the maintenance of calibration records but with the trainee who was learning to maintain the calibration records. The true problem was the method used by the trainee to sort the data in the spreadsheet where the records were stored. In this instance, returning to the master file, sorting the data correctly, and reprinting the required data was simple. In this example, as in others that we could mention, correcting the symptom was easy. But the true problem, this and future trainee's understanding of the software, remained. Therefore, the original fact reported might have been technically correct, but the problem was not accurately identified. In fact, the entire report may be technically correct, management is left with the job of evaluating the validity of each nonconformance and determining how each is to be addressed.

The auditors in this example should have provided some of the additional facts that they collected during the audit, especially since the barebones data could have been misleading. In many cases, auditors already know, or can easily acquire, the additional information needed. Good reports should accurately represent the situation, and each nonconformance should be put in the proper context. You should strive for "quality" reports, not "quantity" of nonconformities (bad facts). The identification of one system weakness is worth 100 pages of minor imperfections found.

Don't Just Report the First Thing That Comes Along. Another bad habit of auditors is to stop investigating at the first defect found. We have observed auditors who look through every record in a file until one nonconformity is found, and then move on to the next item on their checklist. It would appear that the auditor is only interested in reporting the maximum number of nonconformities in as many areas as possible. Auditors who practice such methods are not contributing to the organization, and such actions should not be tolerated by management.

When a nonconformity/defect is found, auditors should record it, and follow through to determine if there is a system/process failure or if the defect only represents a minor flaw in an otherwise excellent system. If every record in a file is examined, the number of actual records examined and the number of nonconforming records should be recorded to indicate the magnitude of the problem. When the audit report is being prepared, the quantifiable data will be invaluable as supporting evidence for the effectiveness or ineffectiveness of the system. Auditors need to continue to collect facts until they determine whether there is an isolated error or a system failure and not stop at the first sign of an imperfection.

An exception to not reporting every imperfection found is the compliance report. Compliance auditing is a necessary evil for regulated industries. To report compliance to a law, regulation, or code, the auditor must report all errors, no matter how small. Compliance reports are singularly focused on demonstrating that a firm is in compliance or not in compliance with a standard. Compliance audits are strictly a control tool of government or independent regulators and are not designed to help the auditee organization. However, this does not prohibit the use of more effective reporting methods that will promote real improvement. (For more information about compliance reporting, refer to the first section of chapter 8, "Compliance Auditing.")

Report On-the-Spot Corrective Action.   A third bad habit of auditors is giving the management/auditee credit for fixing problems on-the-spot. You may say: "Hold on a minute. What's wrong with that?" The problem is that many times systematic problems are hidden because superficial on-the-spot corrections were made. In the previous example about errors in the calibration master list, it would have been a simple matter for management to add the missing equipment to the master list and to re-issue the list prior to completion of the audit, but then effective corrective action would never be taken. Auditors should be very careful before verifying on-the-spot corrective action. Problems should be reported, even if there is on-the-spot correction, when the root cause of the problem is not addressed. We suggest this for the same reason that you would not want a physician to prescribe medication to reduce your headache and fever, when you actually have pneumonia. You may feel somewhat better after taking the medication, but you are still going to die from pneumonia. By the time you discover that something is still wrong, you may very well find that it is too late to act. We would all rather see the problem (pneumonia) be treated, not just the symptoms (the headache and fever). In our own experience (confirmed by internal interviews with other auditors), where the management/auditee was permitted to initiate immediate corrective action to prevent the reporting of a nonconformity, corrective actions are rejected 70 percent of the time because the root cause is not addressed. In other words, on-the-spot corrective actions miss the mark 70 percent of the time.

Ensure Policy is Consistent with Objectives.   Audit organization policy or practice may be contributing to superficial on-the-spot corrective actions. At a meeting, an audit organization registrar complained that almost all the corrective actions submitted by their clients were in the superficial, remedial action category. Yet their own policy allowed the auditor to recommend registration if corrective action was taken on all the nonconformities prior to the audit ending. As a consequence, auditees moved quickly to close out non-conformities during the audit and auditors readily accepted the responses in order to achieve the goal of on-the-spot registration of the quality management system. Somewhere along the way, people lost sight of the goal for an effective quality management system to achieve customer satisfaction. The guidance here is to evaluate your own policy and procedures to ensure that they are not contributing factors to ineffective audit programs.

Use Simple Analytical Tools: Quantify Data.   There are a multitude of methods and tools that auditors can use to analyze data. Most of these tools and methods (scatter diagrams, control charts, histograms, etc.) require more time to use than is available during an audit. However, the auditor can use simple tools to analyze and quantify objective evidence when possible.

Analyzing data can help the auditee understand the importance of an issue identified in the audit. The auditee can use the additional data this provides to make decisions regarding the management of the area audited. Six simple tools that can be easily used are: counting, percentages and ratios, sorting and grouping data, matrices, comparisons, and estimating cost (dollars).

Counting consists of computing a raw number based on observations during the audit. For example: there were 3 findings in the service area; 5 products checked were out of specification; there were 10 units on-hold for rework.

Use of percentages and ratios can enhance the counting data by quantifying it. For example: the service area accounted for 3 of the 5 findings found during the audit; 20% (5/25) of the products checked were out of specification; of 100 units produced, 10/100 (10%) were assigned to be reworked.

Sorting and grouping data can provide additional insight by focusing on problem areas. For example: all 3 findings in the service area concerned the new pump product line (group by product line); 5 products were out of specification for different parameter failures (sort by specification item); all 10 of the items were waiting rework due to a high amperage reading (group by failure code/mode).

Drawing matrices provides additional visual representation of the data collected by sorting and grouping. For example: the product identification numbers could be listed in the left hand column and the failed specification parameters in a row across the top; the 10 items awaiting rework could be listed in the left hand column and the failure codes in a row across the top.

Comparisons of other areas, products, product lines, or time periods can point to system problems. For example: the other lines did not have any units on hold waiting rework; the other products lines had the same level of on-hold items waiting rework; last month an average of two units were on hold at any particular time. With this last piece of information the auditor could compute the percentage increase in items on hold from month to month.

Determining the dollars at risk due to the problem identified during the audit is the most powerful information, and possibly the hardest to quantify. If the auditor knows the average cost of rework, the auditor could report the cost of the higher rework levels. If there is not Cost of Quality system, the auditor can ask for cost data from the auditee. Frequent use of these six simple tools to analyze data will add significant value to your audit report.

Consider the Situation: System Failure versus System Immaturity. Auditors should be diligent when conducting a quality system audit. Diligence should be focused on demonstrating the degree of system effectiveness, not perfection. You may say that system effectiveness is evidenced by the presence of or absence of nonconformities, but that simply is not true. Instead, a search for nonconformities proves imperfection, not system failure. The imperfections found may merely be an indication of system immaturity or that the associates are learning to apply new principles, but hardly system failure.

For example, let's say an organization has determined that its current quality system does not meet the needs of its customers and decides to implement ISO 9001. This organization prepares a quality manual, procedures, and work instructions that are in compliance with this quality system standard. Then you, the auditor, arrive on the scene to conduct a quality system audit. You will find that two things are very evident:

- There is not enough evidence to prove the system is "in compliance."
- The associates do not fully understand all the requirements.

If you are surprised, shocked, dismayed, and thoroughly disgusted with the progress of this organization, then you have not evaluated the system.

However, if you take the time to evaluate progress of the system as a whole, you will find that the organization is not yet perfect, but is taking steps in the right direction. You will find that there is not enough evidence yet to prove that all the procedures are effective and that the associates have not implemented all the requirements—not yet, at any rate. This is a natural part of an organization's learning curve, and it should be expected. If you determine that the system needs time to develop, you should return in six months. Upon your return, you should find that there has been significant improvement. It is important for auditors to consider the quality system maturity when reporting the results of the investigation. An audit report that does not properly represent the status of a recently implemented quality management system can demoralize an organization at a critical time of development. Similarly an audit report that does not properly represent the status of a fully tested mature system can result in overconfidence in management and inaccurate assessment of business risk.

Although audit reports may be correct, they may not be an effective tool or aid for identification of important problems that need the attention of management. A correct report does not mean it is a clear report. Some audit reports are just gobbledygook.

Prepare Clear Reports: User Friendly and Understandable.   You shouldn't need to consult a technical dictionary to figure out what the report means. Too many auditors either try to impress management with their technical vocabulary or have poor written communication skills, so they hide behind an impressive vocabulary. A report can sound important, yet an interpreter will be needed to understand what it means. For example:

- The product encapsulators in the logistics area center were inadvertently altered by random mutilation of exterior covering in violation of specification 111.344 and specification 121.566.

- Quality system reference documents contained in the JPR Industries Standard Operating Procedures Manual, dated November 6, 1995; Issue 3; Section 17.345 preclude requirements for issue amendment levels stipulated in procedure 5005, dated June 18, 1994; section 5.456.

- Units were found to be in violation of procedure 9901 and disregarding specification RE001, causing an infraction.

Tips for Clear Reports.   Audit reports should be user friendly so that the reader can easily understand what is being reported.

- The auditor should use terminology that the document user will understand. Simple language is always better. There are times when the use of a four- or five-syllable word is more appropriate, but this is rare. We have found that most individuals (even those who are highly technically oriented) do not have a sufficient command of higher-level words to understand what is being said. We have presented information in classes, with everyone nodding in agreement (not nodding off), and then asked a couple of questions about what was just said and found that everyone missed the point. The information was reviewed using simpler terms that the students could relate to, then they understood it. In a recent movie, a lawyer would fluster other lawyers in court proceedings by asking them to explain what they said in terms that a five-year-old could understand (sounds like a good guideline to us).

- Auditors should avoid acronyms when possible. We would be willing to bet that if you ask the CEO about the condition of his CARs, the CEO is likely to glance at the parking lot. On the other hand, the quality assurance manager would more likely think of corrective action requests. J. P. recently purchased a new computer that has one of those cards the size of a credit card and couldn't remember its acronym until he was told (tongue-in-check) that PCMCIA stood for "People Can't Memorize Computer Industry Acronyms." Now the manufacturers have dropped the six-character acronym altogether and just call them PC cards.

- Auditors should be direct and to the point, with no padding and no flowery language. Managers are busy and do not want their time wasted, so audit reports should get right to the bottom line. We have read 10-page reports stating how wonderful everything is and how wonderful the people are; at the bottom of page 11, management finds out what the problems are. Some auditors believe that if they pad (soften) their audit reports, the auditee will not notice that the auditor has pointed out serious problems. To pad reports is unprofessional. It is okay to point out good qualities, but don't abuse it or the report will not be taken seriously.

- Auditors should use a standard format if it improves communication with the auditee. Standard report formats make it easier for the auditor to be consistent and easier for the auditee to make comparisons from audit to audit. There are no hard and fast rules here, but there are definite advantages for quality improvement. In a survey[2], 50 percent of the respondents indicated that they modified their procedures as an activity to improve the overall effectiveness of the audit report. One survey participant responded with: *Audit customers asked for a common approach and report formats. Our procedure was modified based on those customer requests.*

- Auditors should reference requirements or objectives in their report that are not being fulfilled. This improves communication by allowing traceability to the requirement or business objective.

- Auditors should define unfamiliar terms used in the audit report. There are many terms that have different meanings in different environments (for example: nonconformance, fact, defect, noncompliance, concern, observation, finding, improvement point, etc.). Terms should be defined in the report or in other documents available to the auditee (such as a procedure). It seems that the new whiz kids of software and the internet are creating new words every day. If you don't make them explain, they will simply talk over your head.

The basic requirement is that the users (the audit customers) understand the report. If auditees have a lot of questions about what the report means, it is not clear.

We know of one situation in which two auditors were complaining about a recent audit. Apparently, there were fireworks at the exit meeting and everyone was upset. Over dinner, the two auditors consoled themselves by stating that the auditee/management was too stupid or ignorant to understand the pearls of wisdom in their audit report. The auditors' attitude is appalling. Auditors need to get rid of their historical baggage and strive to maintain a positive, proactive customer attitude. When people have new ideas and want to change things, or if they find things wrong with the status quo, they must sell their ideas to those with the authority to change the system. Why should auditors be any different?

Effective Reporting

Reports can only be effective if they help, not hinder, improvement efforts. Reports should be organized and written in a way that promotes improvement. You must continually utilize the information and technology available to enhance reports to be more effective, as an instrument for progress. Audit reports should not be stagnant, but should be vibrant, dynamic, "jump off the paper and grab you" information. It takes some work, but it can be done.

For example, J. P. conducted an audit of a company that was registered to an ISO 9001 standard. When he finished presenting the audit report at the exit meeting, a couple of people started to clap. He was flabbergasted, since he had just spent about 45 minutes telling them about their problems. The applause quickly died down because it didn't seem appropriate considering the occasion. However, his report had hit a nerve, and that company's attitude toward quality auditing changed from that point forward. Getting applause for an audit report was probably a once-in-a-lifetime occurrence, and he still gets goose bumps when he thinks about it.

Reporting problems to the auditee and then putting them in writing is the most difficult part of an audit. It requires skill and patience, because if done wrong the report most certainly will not result in improvement. There are several options for phrasing what is being reported. The method chosen to report the results will depend on the organization being audited (what is most effective) and the purpose of the audit. The reporting of problems is both the product of the audit and the input to the improvement process. We have already stated that the facts collected (the factual evidence) must be correct.

A tremendous amount of time and effort was expended to get to the report-writing stage of the audit. At this point all the lead auditor has is a badly mangled checklist, a dog-eared audit plan, a pile of notes, copies of documents that are supposed to represent evidence, and several tired auditors. Converting this meaningless heap into a worthwhile product can be a real challenge for the lead auditor and the audit team. In the following sections we discuss options for reporting the results of the investigation. One of the most common approaches used in the ISO world is the reporting of nonconformities.

Phrasing the Problem

Nonconformity Statements

The reporting of nonconformities is a recognized convention used by third-party organizations. Although it has its complexities, it is a relatively simple method. Audit organizations will generate lists of nonconformities. A nonconformity is the nonfulfillment of a (specified) requirement.[3]

When using the nonconformity approach, the audit report becomes a series of nonconformity statements. Each nonconformity statement must be a complete thought, a sentence that expresses an assertion. The statement may be one sentence or several sentences long, whatever is needed to make the point. The nonconformity statement should refer to objective evidence collected to support the reporting of a nonfulfillment of a requirement. A requirement is stated in a document, such as a performance standard (ISO 9001, QS-9000, quality award criteria, quality manual, procedures, work instructions) that the organization has adopted. Requirements may also come from customers, regulators, local officials, and other parties interested in regulating or doing business with the organization.

The ABC's for a proper nonconformity statement area are:

A. State the unfulfilled requirement.

B. If not clear, explain why the factual evidence is a violation of the requirement.

C. Reference the requirement.

Examples of nonconformance statements:

1. Several lots of product found in the distribution area contained nonconforming product (damaged packaging) and were not identified or segregated as required by SOP 1505, Section 7.

   A. Nonconforming product was not identified or segregated.

   B. Several lots in the distribution area contained unidentified nonconforming product.

   C. Reference: SOP 1505, Section 7.

2. The existing document control system does not provide for adequate control of revision levels. During the audit several different versions of the audit procedure were being used in violation of ISO 9001, clause 5.

   A. Document revisions are not being controlled.

   B. Several versions of the same procedure are being used.

   C. Reference: ISO 9001, clause 5.5.

3. Several units ready for customer acceptance (use) were nonconforming to specified readiness requirements (were not properly cleaned). Specification 1122.

   A. Units were not properly prepared.

   B. Several units were nonconforming to specified readiness requirements for being cleaned.

   C. Reference: Specification 1122.

Typical phrases used including the following:

- There was no system for . . .
- There was no evidence to confirm . . . which had not been . . .
- The existing system does not provide for . . .

The statements are true, but not very robust. In Items #1 and #3, it is not clear what several means. In Item #2, we are not sure whether this applies only to the audit procedure or if there are other documents where the issue level is not controlled. Based on the nonconformance statements, we are not sure if these are systemic problems or isolated events.

Classification of Nonconformances. Many audit organizations further classify nonconformities as major or minor. Nonconformances are classified as *minor* if they do not represent a breakdown of the quality system nor directly result in a nonconforming product or service. A minor nonconformance (for example, a documentation error or a single observation) has little negative consequence to the organization or customer of the organization. Several similar minor nonconformities could result in one major nonconformance.

Nonconformances are classified as *major* if they represent an absence or breakdown of a quality system control (element) or result in nonconforming product or service being supplied to the customer. Some organizations classify nonconformances as category 1 (major) or 2 (minor) similar to hurricane ratings (categories). A major nonconformity could be quality records or no corrective action on audit findings.

The nonconformity classification is a risk assessment. High risk may be that the organization's quality system is not in compliance with higher level documents (such as ISO 9001, QS-9000, AS 9000, TS 9000, etc.) or that nonconforming product or service will be supplied to the customer. Minor nonconformities represent low risk. Nonconformity statements and their classification serve a useful purpose to assess the degree of continuous compliance to regulations or to standards adopted by the organization. However, there is no implication or linkage that a major nonconformity is a systemic problem. In most cases a major nonconformity is simply a nonfulfillment of a requirement that has a higher risk (as normally defined by the auditing organization). This is a qualitative analysis of the nonconformities identified during the investigation. The possible exception is when multiple minor nonconformities are grouped to create one major nonconformity. Grouping similar minor nonconformities would be using quantitative analysis to determine what is reported and how. Even when quantitative analysis techniques are used, most nonconformity statements just describe the symptoms, not the problem to be solved. For the preceding reasons, nonconformity statements have a very limited positive effect in promoting a change in the business or quality system. The use of nonconformance statements requires management to struggle with the issues to figure out the extent of the problem. Naturally, because it takes more effort, most people are going to take the easy way out—therefore, no improvement occurs.

To overcome some of the weaknesses of reporting nonconformities, management should analyze audit results using the following techniques and those described in chapter 2 entitled Reason/Pain Matrix.

For regulators and registrars the reporting of conformance or compliance better suits the requirements of the conformity assessment process. However, internal audits and supplier assessments have a lot more flexibility and we recommend using the findings approach discussed in the next section. It is more difficult, but the benefits to the organization will be much greater.

Put It in a Finding

Nonconformities tend to point out inconsistencies in the way things are documented or minor discrepancies in the way a function was intended to function. For example, a procedure may state that a particular operation will be conducted according to the steps outlined in a work instruction. Yet, during an audit, you find that the operation is not conducted as described by the work instruction. This could be anything from omitting steps in the process to failing to complete the specified form. Although this must be recorded, it is not an indication that the system has failed. If this is all that is reported to management, the response may be: "So what?" Management needs more from an audit than a list of minor inconsistencies or symptoms of problems. In order to satisfy those needs, auditors must identify the system concerns, which are stated as findings. A finding, according to the dictionary, is the "results of an investigation." Dennis Arter takes it a step further and defines it as follows:[4]

> Finding: An audit conclusion that identifies a condition that has a significant adverse effect on the quality of the goods and services produced. An audit finding contains both cause and effect and is normally accompanied by several specific examples of the observed condition.

You should also consider the following definition which we believe is straight forward and links findings to organizational objectives.

Finding: An audit conclusion based on objective evidence stating a system weakness related to organizational objectives.

System concerns are determined by analyzing the evidence found during the audit. When this is done, you will find that the evidence (observations, data) can be grouped into like categories. By this we mean more than the fact that there will be a "group" of observations under "Inspection and Testing" for example, or a specific section or topic. The relationships between evidence observed must be identified so that they may be put in their natural grouping and the sum of their symptomatic effect can be stated as a finding. We like to think of it as looking for the common thread that links the various facts collected. For example, the following nonconformities were recorded in an actual audit:

Case 1:

1. Product samples in the storage area are not identified in any manner.

2. Process sheets indicate material which failed the stated test requirements is passed without authorization or comment.

3. The Final Test Plan/Procedure does not specify that finished product shall have passed earlier inspections and tests.

4. Nonconforming material in storage areas are not clearly identified as to status.

5. Paragraph 4.6 of NCP 213.012 states that the Technical Manager is responsible for the disposition of nonconforming material in contradiction with paragraph 4.2 of the same document.

6. The disposition of material in NCP 213.012, 4.8 lists three (3) options for disposition, yet the Material Review Board Report lists five (5) options.

7. Product in the nonconforming material storage is not identified.

8. The table for classification of materials for RPT process is blank (IC 206.003, 4.7).

9. The methods for periodic verification of materials in procedure IC 206.003,4.8, are undefined.

10. There are no procedures for control of customer supplied product, yet it is reported that one customer provides materials for processing and return.

The audit team stated the system effect of these nonconformities in a finding as:

> *Finding 1: Material is not adequately identified to ensure that only materials meeting the customer's requirements are used.*

The Case 1 finding has some shortcomings, such as the use of acronyms, and it may not be clear to the reader if "product" is finished product or incoming product or goods. However, we have been assured that each fact was fully explained to the site representative and to management at the exit meeting. The important point is that the audit team pulled together 10 facts out of 40 nonconformities that represented a system problem, not just a random list of defects.

Case 2:

> Background: The company produces a liquid product that has a high value added. Most product is sold in large drums, but a portion of the production is sold in small specialty containers at a high price.
>
> 1. There is no procedure for packaging (repackaging) of small containers (specialty orders and product samples).
> 2. The part drums (partially filled) used to fill small containers (specialty orders) are not controlled and a vent bung was missing from one drum. This lack of control could result in contaminated or deteriorated product being shipped out for special package orders or as samples to be tested by customers.
> 3. The canning operation is not addressed in the quality manual nor in any third-level procedure.
> 4. The balances (scales) used for can weighing were either beyond the required calibration date or were never calibrated.
> 5. There is no procedure for periodic checking of can weights.
> 6. There is no procedure requirement to mix drums (material stratifies) prior to repackaging.
> 7. Material (finished product) is left in the canning machine between runs. The current product has been in the canning machine for two days (note: material has a shelf life limit).
> 8. The top of the canning machine was covered with a piece of cardboard and there was no indication what product was in the machine.
> 9. There is no procedure for the safe filling of inflammables. The electrical equipment in the area was not rated for hazardous atmospheres.

10. The small filled containers stored (available for shipment) in the area were rusty and dirty. Area personnel stated that it is common practice (though not written) to repackage any damaged or deteriorated product containers prior to shipment.

The audit team deduced the following from the 10 facts:

> Finding 2: *The scope of the controls in the warehouse area does not extend to the small packaging (canning) operation. This can lead to poor-quality product (off-specification product, off-weight packages, deteriorated packaging) being sent to customers.*

Reporting the effect of the nonconformities as done in Cases 1 and 2 provides management with an audit conclusion about a system weakness, supported by evidence (facts collected during the audit). An audit or assessment is a more effective tool for improvement if it assists the auditee (the customer of the audit) in addressing systematic errors. The audit report should not just be technically correct, but should clearly identify system concerns of importance to the customers of the audit: client, auditee, internal customers, and external customers. In Cases 1 and 2, the important issues that need to be addressed (keeping stuff identified, making sure specialty container packaging is under control) are pointed out to management. Also, management knows the problems are probably costing them money as well as customer goodwill.

If this technique seems too complex, findings can be created using one of the quality management tools. Affinity diagrams can be used to organize evidence into natural groupings or relationships. In a classroom, record all the evidence on Post-It™ notes. Place the notes on the floor or wall. Then ask the teams to sort the evidence into natural groupings. Outliers and isolated evidence (does not seem to relate to groups) should be identified. Additional note cards should be created if evidence fits in more than one group. Next, write a finding for each group. The finding should include the control, the problem reason, and its effect on the organization. After chapter 2, a model will be presented that can be used to write finding statements.

Summary

Your goal should be to promote auditor practices that facilitate the audit process while improving the effectiveness of corrective action process that results from the investigation. These include:

- Investigate nonconformities thoroughly.
- Do not report laundry lists of nonconformities.

- Summarize evidence in findings.
- Do not accept immediate corrective actions at face value.
- Analyze data in order to report the disease, not the symptom.
- Provide audit reports that clearly identify system concerns.

The purpose of the audit is to aid the auditee in addressing systematic errors. The audit report should not just be technically correct, but should clearly identify system concerns of importance to the customers (client, auditee, internal customers, and external customers).

Don't model your internal and supplier audit reports after third-party audit organizations. Their agenda is different from yours.

Audits can be a valuable tool for management, but if the information is not properly conveyed, the auditor is part of the organization's problem, not part of the solution. Many excellent auditors do not challenge themselves enough to provide the value-added reporting that is needed for real improvement. Audits, assessments, and examinations are one of the primary inputs into the corrective/preventive action process.

Chapter 2

Reason-Pain Matrix

Relate to Customer Interests

We ended chapter 1 with nonconformity and finding statements. As well written as those statements may be, it is not enough. Auditors and quality managers must find a way to explain why auditees should take their valuable time to address the results of the audit. What better way than to explain in terms of dollars they may either gain or lose?

Findings are frequently stated in terms of the requirements of a standard. However, if the benefits to the internal and external customers are not evident, there may be some reluctance on the part of management to act on these findings. The lead auditor should ensure that the audit team identifies important reasons for management to want to correct this system failure prior to the exit meeting.

In the finding statements that ended the previous chapter, we used the word *customer* in facts and in the finding statements when applicable. Since management is interested in keeping existing customers and adding new customers, the focus on customer satisfaction shows that the auditor is truly interested in what's important to the organization rather than pointing out all their failures and imperfections. You are probably asking: "How can I come up with my own findings?" It is not easy and it will require a lot more thought than reporting a simple list. It may take two to four times longer to come up with good finding statements, but the effort is well worth it.

The audit team must analyze the facts, the nonconformities for which there is supporting evidence, found during the audit. You will need to use judgment along with utilization of some analytical tools. You can group, trend, calculate, chart, and diagram information. This is the hardest part of effective problem identification. There is no one right answer, nor is there one right model. You have a list of facts and must determine if there are common threads woven among the facts that will point out systematic problems (problems with the system or process of how business is conducted). You must use your judgment based on your knowledge of the process and your experience. It is like the word puzzles where a scrambled list of letters is provided and you must rearrange the letters to form a word or words.

Identify the Reason and the Pain

Auditors and managers may use the Reason-Pain (RP) matrix as a tool for linking audit results with customer (auditee) interests.

We can start construction of the matrix by determining the reason for reporting a problem, defect, or nonconformance. We propose that reasons for problems fit into three categories:

R1: Not defined (documented or other means): the system or process (how you do things) has not been designed to meet requirements. Requirements may be found in quality management standards, customer requirements, award criteria or organizational objectives. *A management control is needed, but there is none.* For example: there is no established method or process of handling customer complaints.

R2: Not implemented: the system or process is properly designed (designed to meet requirements) but is not properly implemented or deployed. People have not been trained, informed, or the message was not accepted because people will not change or the change doesn't make any sense. People are not doing what they are supposed to do. *A management control has been developed but no one follows it.* For example: there is a procedure for recording and responding to customer complaints but either people are not following it or are unaware of it.

R3: Does not meet objectives: the system/process meets requirements and is implemented/deployed, but the outcomes (output, results) are not consistent with achievement of the overall objective(s). A method is defined and people are following it, but it does not meet objectives (quality or business). *The management control is being followed but is not effective.* For example: the procedure is so cumbersome that at best it takes one week to respond to a customer complaint and now there are complaints about the complaint system.

Another example of an R3 reason happened during the audit of the process for controlling nonconforming material. There was a method and it was being followed. When the auditor asked to see the records, the auditee reported that by their definition of nonconforming product (must be a customer return), there were no reports of nonconforming material. The auditor knew that as much as 50 percent of the production was nonconforming and being reworked. The auditee refused to recognize the existence of nonconforming material, and therefore circumvented the primary objective of the management control.

The three reasons for reporting problems match with three audit objectives. These are: (1) to determine adequacy of the designed system, (2) that the system is implemented and maintained, and (3) the system is effective and will achieve organizational objectives.

Next, the organizational pain from the problems can also be put into three categories. In other words, management's interests can be classified into three core (COR) categories. They are:

P1: Cost: Addressing the problem leads to lower overhead cost, lower direct unit costs (cost of goods sold), and improved efficiency (productivity) for the organization. If sales remain the same and costs (expenses) can be reduced per unit, there will be increased profit. Figure 2.1 shows how lowering cost will increase net income.

P2: Opportunity: Addressing the problem leads to new products, opens new markets, adds new services, and increases capacity that will increase the wealth of the organization (such as decreased capital spending, increased sales, etc.). Every good business person is constantly searching for opportunities. Opportunities normally represent a significant increase in net income either by increasing revenue (new markets, new products) or identifying a major capacity increase with little or no corresponding capital cost. For example: finding a use (customer) for a by-product that was being dumped.

P3: Risk: Addressing the problem reduces the risk to the organizational/ business wealth. There's risk of a fine, violation, or negative publicity, or that customers may go elsewhere (customer satisfaction). Risk

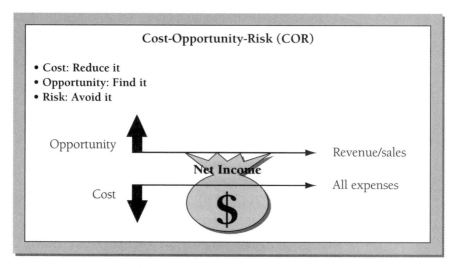

Figure 2.1. Cost-Opportunity-Risk (COR).

of a fine, court judgment, and/or loss of license are quantifiable. Risk of losing customers is very elusive and normally hidden by new customer sales. I have never seen a sales manager report that sales were up 15 percent but could have been 18 percent if it wasn't for the snafus last year.

Management will be interested in correcting problems that are linked to Cost-Opportunity-Risk. If problems found cannot be linked to Cost-Opportunity-Risk, then management may decide they are not important. For example: if we take the facts from the Case 1 audit (page 21) and sort by reason and pain (cause and effect), we will get the matrix shown in Table 2.1.

There were more than 40 different facts observed during the Case 1 audit. The 10 facts in the matrix were selected (grouped) to represent a system problem (a common thread). From the R/P matrix you can see that the most common reason for the failures is poor implementation (deployment) of the process. Now, looking at the pain (P1, P2, and P3), you can see that productivity and customer satisfaction are benefits to the organization if the problem is fixed. With this insight you can strengthen the finding statement:

Material identification controls have not been effectively implemented to ensure that only materials meeting the customer's requirements are used, resulting in productivity losses and potential customer dissatisfaction.

#	Bad fact	Reason/cause			Pain/effect			Comments— errors and opportunity
		Design not adequate for control, R1	Not imple- mented, R2	Does not meet objectives, R3	Cost, P1	Oppor- tunity for greater wealth, P2	Risk to wealth, P3	
1	Product sample not identified		░		$			Cannot trace samples/ extra work to verify
2	Failed material passed on w/o authorization		░				$	Bad material may be used
3	Procedure doesn't require that product pass all tests	░					$	Risk that bad material is used
4	NC material status not identified		░				$	Risk that wrong material is used
5	Disposition by tech manager, or ?	░					$	Communication/ control risk
6	NCP three options, MRB five options?		░				$	Communication/ control risk
7	NC product not identified in storage		░		$		$	Risk that wrong product is used/extra sorting
8	RPT process table is blank		░				$	Communication/ control risk
9	Materials verification method undefined	░			$$			Controls unde- fined resulting in duplication
10	Customer- supplied product not identified		░	░	$$		$$$	Major customer is unhappy

Table 2.1. R/P matrix for Case 1.

Wow, it looks like this is important! This problem needs to be addressed right away. A list of individual defects will not promote change to the system, but a well-designed finding statement will induce changes in how business is conducted.

The R/P matrix links causes of failure (problems) with the pain to the organization, the cause/effect relationship. We suggest that if there is no pain to the organization, the finding does not need to be fixed, except for your personal satisfaction or third-party (outsider) requirements.

Now look at the Case 2 R/P matrix (Table 2.2) and point out the pain of each nonconformity (bad fact).

We can start by asking why management would even be interested in the small volume packaging line. After all, 98 percent of everything goes through the main line, which seems to be operating just fine. The big deal about the small line is that they fill specialty packaging orders and charge about 10 times (on a pound basis) more than standard product pricing. That means that the small line accounts for, not 2 percent, but 17 percent of the revenue generated. Secondly, marketing/sales request new customer and product samples be sent from the small packaging operation. The sample service supplied by the distribution department is one of the sales department's major marketing costs (they want value for their money like anyone else). With this background, let's discuss the management hot buttons for each nonconformance (bad fact).

Analysis and Comment

1. Having no procedure for packaging is interesting, but no one said it was being done wrong. There could be some inefficiencies and they know the line costs (price per pound—$/lb) are very high.

2. Evidence that specialty and sample order product could be contaminated is alarming, because: (1) specialty order customers (the ones that purchase high profit margin product) could be getting inferior product, and (2) new customers or new product evaluations could be (have been) jeopardized. The final step in getting new customers and products approved hinges on sample quality.

3. The fact that this process is not mentioned in the quality manual is sort of a ho-hum fact for management.

4. Evidence that container weights are not controlled worries management for two reasons. One of the key reasons for customers to purchase small containers is that the customer

#	Bad fact	Ref.	Reason/cause			Pain/effect			Comments— errors and opportunity
			Design not adequate for control, R1	Not implemented, R2	Does not meet objectives, R3	Cost, P1	Opportunity for greater wealth, P2	Risk to wealth, P3	
1	No Procedure for packing small containers		▓			$		$	Process not optimized, done wrong
2	Part drums not protected authorization				▓			$	Contaminated product may be used
3	Not in quality manual		▓					$	Risk that important process not controlled
4	Scales not checked			▓				$$	Risk of wrong weight, yield customer dissatisfaction
5	No verification controls for weight?		▓					$	No assurance targets are achieved
6	No procedure for mixing		▓		▓	$$		$	Customer gets bad product: redo and rework
7	Material left in machine			▓		$		$	Yield and customer complaints; lose customer
8	Product in machine not identified			▓				$	Customer gets bad material to use
9	No procedure for harzadous material		▓					$$$	The place could burn down: code violation
10	Rusty cans			▓	▓	$$$		$	Refilling and replacing: customer complains

Table 2.2. R/P matrix for Case 2.

wants the material pre-dosed so that they do not need to weigh it themselves. This could be causing the customer problems in their operation that they are not aware of and could lead to customer complaints, especially since package weights are easy to check. Every complaint costs money to follow-up, and with every complaint there is a probability that the customer will go elsewhere (loss of customer satisfaction). The second reason management is concerned is yield—they could be giving away product. In this case, the yield issue is less important because specialty orders only represent 2 percent of the volume sold.

5. The fact that there is no procedure for verification of can weights is interesting in view of the above, but not linked to major pain factors. If the auditors asked the people in the area to do some check weighing and found lots of variation, then this fact would become more important (stronger linkage to COR).

6. No procedure issue again, and again sort of a ho-hum fact, except that this material stratifies. If it is not properly mixed, the customers would observe significant variability in the product received. Customers could complain, and if product must be repackaged, this represents rework and affects productivity goals—the small packaging operation is already considered one of the least productive areas in the facility. The next thing to find out is how much repackaging takes place and how much material is wasted (disposal costs are high).

We will stop here because we're sure you get the idea. The more you know about the business and management hot buttons, the more effective the audit report will be. Management will want to take corrective action and fix the problem before there is a major crisis. If the organization is losing one out of 20 new customers due to the evaluation of a bad sample, it could represent a million dollars in revenue lost each year. You can also make an R/P matrix of all the facts collected from an audit sorted by area, system, process, or topic.

An analysis of an entire quality system using an R/P matrix revealed the following:

• The purchasing department designed its system but is not communicating what people should do. This is an across-the-board, systematic problem within the purchasing department. If resolved, many of the issues in purchasing could save money for the organization.

- Many of the problems in manufacturing relate to the failure to meet quality and operational objectives (even though they have controls in place). These gaps risk the organization's wealth by affecting customer satisfaction (potential customer complaints). Information is not being properly recorded that is needed to satisfy codes and regulations.

- In the sales and marketing area, a number of issues were revealed dealing with inadequate controls to meet performance standard requirements. Through personal knowledge the auditor knew that these were important, but minor.

- Regarding corrective action, there was no formal system for analyzing records. The company functioned in a reactive mode. A system needs to be put in place to be proactive.

- The auditor could not detect an overall weakness in the company using the matrix. In general, there is adequate commitment to the system and for improvement; however, some department/area weaknesses need to be addressed.

This type of matrix analysis helps to better understand the weakness within the organization. Once you have created an R/P matrix a few times, you will start to think in a manner to associate cause and effect with COR. Construction of an R/P matrix must be combined with personal knowledge and intuitive reasoning to provide a proper analysis report. The R/P matrix can be used by auditors, audit program managers, corrective action teams, and top management to analyze and understand needs.

Quality Costs and the R/P Matrix

The dollar signs under the pain columns in Table 2.2 relate to actual and potential losses to the organization. Traditional quality cost or cost-of-poor-quality systems could fill in some of the dollar answers, but few quality cost systems are daring enough to include all potential losses to an organization. Many quality cost systems focus on easily identifiable costs and expenses.

Traditional quality costs are comprised of the following:

- Prevention costs: new product/service review, design review, quality planning, supplier assessment, quality improvement team meetings, quality system audits, quality process audits, process capability studies, education, and training.

- Appraisal costs: incoming inspection, source inspection, product/service audits (to verify a product or service meets requirements), compliance audits (product and process), testing, test equipment, and calibration of test equipment.
- Failure (internal and external) costs: scrap, rework, reinspection, retesting, sorting, regrading, processing customer complaints, claims, recalls, redo, returns, etc.

The total cost and potential cost to an organization should include:

- potential loss of orders from existing customers (lost profit)
- loss of future customers (lost profit)
- savings from capital investment avoidance or delay in capital spending
- avoiding potential claims, potential citations and regulatory costs
- interest saved due to reductions in working capital cost (the money needed to operate the organization on a daily basis)
- productivity losses for rescheduling, replanning, reorganizing

Often, estimated internal costs are too low. A good reality check is to ask an outside organization to do the rework or provide the service and compare their costs to your estimated costs.

Every organization should know how much a customer complaint costs. You will be very surprised at how much a dissatisfied customer is costing the organization. To figure out the average cost of a customer complaint, conduct a study and follow several representative complaints (minor issues, major issues). Then add up the out-of-pocket costs and internal productivity and equipment costs. To do this effectively, one must visualize how the organization would function if all customers were always satisfied. Here are some suggestions for collecting your own product complaint cost. A product complaint, by our definition, had to deal with a specification or performance issue.

The following is a complaint cost collection plan:

1. Flow chart the apparent complaint process.
2. Review complaint records.
3. Interview customer service, the complaint coordinator, and inventory clerk to verify process and actions for various complaints.
4. Interview the marketing and product management personnel to verify the process and actions for specified complaints. The

business area should also know the cost structure and scope of the complaint program.

5. Trace several complaints to include a minor complaint and a major complaint (use complaint records).

6. Then calculate the full cost (hourly rate, benefits, and overhead allocations) of the following resources:

    • Customer service and complaint coordinator

    • Cost of entering data into the computer (data entry charge out rate needed to pay for the computer hardware, software and maintenance)

    • Technical service cost to review and to conduct tests

    • Follow-up sales call

    • Marketing department/ manager cost (time)

    • Product manager cost, tracking cost

    • Calls to Plant quality control (QC)

    • Conference calls

    • Special customer instruction cost

    • Price adjustments or other customer give-a-ways

    • Special trip cost for top management to visit customer

Then you can do the same thing for distribution function (for example, late shipments, damage in transit, etc.). Don't be surprised if the average complaint cost is several thousand dollars. However, one must remember that customer complaint costs will vary from organization to organization due to the type of product and type of market. You don't need an official quality cost system to be able to point out the pain of nonconformities. A quality cost system is neither adequate to identify all potential losses (risks) to the organization nor is it flexible enough to apply to each and every situation. In Table 2.2, Case 2 R/P matrix Item 10, the existence of rusty product sample cans was cited as a nonconformity. Sending out product in rusty cans for possible new applications or for potential customers to evaluate could have a huge impact on the organization's profitability. If there were only a slight chance that the rusty can would contribute to a "no" decision by a potential customer, it could result in hundreds of thousands of dollars lost due to sales/marketing/research productivity and missed sales opportunities (loss of future profits). However, when making observations during the audit and interviewing the packaging personnel, they indicated that all rusty cans (as judged by the packer) are repackaged. In this case the impact on the organization shifts to the cost of repackaging (marked as $$$) and a much lower risk of an occasional subpar can being sent out (marked as $). People often ask: "How do you get these numbers?" The answer is, ask the people who should know.

Once a problem is identified via the system audit, it is management's job to assess the cost versus benefit: the cost of preventing the problem compared to the actual and potential losses for doing nothing. Simply: "What is the cost of doing nothing versus the cost of prevention?" Benefits to the 'for profit' organization can be increased net income due to lower cost or additional sales to existing or new customers. Benefits to the 'not-for-profit' organization can increase customer satisfaction or additional capacity with same resources (budget).

Our objective in using the R/P matrix is to provide a tool to help point out weaknesses and strengths in management systems and place some level of importance to the findings.

Don't Forget Intuitive Analysis (Perceived Importance)

We constantly use our intuitive ability to sort out and identify important problems. Intuitive analysis is far superior to other methods because our brain kicks into gear and analyzes issues against the total sum of our knowledge of a situation. The brain knows what is going on today, what is important to the company, the problems encountered, and the goals. The brain can also take into account the informal controls and cultural issues within an organization. A colleague believes that the use of intuitive abilities comes best from the heart, not the brain. For best results, decisions should be based on heart qualities or how you feel about something. The drawback to intuitive analysis is that (1) it depends solely on the motivation of the individual; (2) sometimes we don't see the forest for the trees; and (3) the quality of the output is based heavily on the individual's background and life experiences (and whether our internal receiver was turned on during those experiences).

The best approach is to combine the use of analytical tools (cause-and-effect diagram, flowcharts, R/P matrix) with intuition. You may know the old saying: "There are lies, damn lies, and statistics." Raw statistics are frequently erroneous because the wrong assumptions were made, background information was not provided, or the wrong measures were reported. Remember to always ask yourself: "Does this make sense based on what I know?"

Use Management Terminology

Auditors should use terms that the customer of the audit will understand. Fellow auditors and quality professionals are usually not the audit customers. If the audit is a service that auditors have been hired to perform, then the report is the tangible result of the service (assessing or examining) performed or the product left with the customer. Who are the audit customers? Who are the people involved in the process and what are their needs? You would not be pleased if a lawyer only spoke to you in legalese, and management is no less pleased when audit results are reported in terms that are not clear, concise, and meaningful to the organization as a whole.

Bottom-Line Tutorial

Auditors don't need to be financial wizards, but they should know something about how money is accounted for. If auditors do not understand how the money yardstick is calibrated, it is difficult to effectively point out organizational pain. Auditors should be familiar with what makes up the following:

Terms used to manage resources include:

- Profit-and-loss statements
- Balance sheet
- Discounted cash flow
- How overhead costs are allocated and what is included in overhead costs
- Variable and fixed costs
- Wealth and equity
- Direct and indirect labor costs
- Capital spending (discretionary and nondiscretionary)
- The cost of capital

Organization performance measures include:

- Yield and rate calculations
- Cycle time
- Inventory turnover and working capital
- Pay back
- Return on investment (ROI) and Return on Equity (ROE)
- Profit margin
- Earnings per share

If these terms are Greek to you, then you need to do some self-study or attend a local college course on financial management.

Auditors' Universal Fallback Position: Do It or Else!

We have observed many auditors using an old fallback position to motivate management into taking findings seriously. They say: "You gotta do it because the standard says so." This tactic falls on deaf ears and promotes negative feelings about auditors and the entire audit process. Some auditors use this approach as the primary motivation to get things done, and others use it as a fallback position when they get frustrated with the auditee (the customer of the audit). The "standard says so" motivation to do something comes off as "the sky is falling." All too often, managers hear justifications such as: "You must do it this way because it's in the procedure, because of the tax codes, because accounting said so," etc. A manager should not blindly follow the written word if it is detrimental to the organization.

Operations managers are paid to make decisions about how resources will be used to assure continued profitability and survival of the organization. An implied threat by an auditor is the last thing they want to hear. Management's response is likely to be the opposite of what was intended. Management may respond with: "What must we do to get around it? What is the absolute minimum that has to be done?" "We will deal with it when it comes up." Or management may seek a second opinion that will, of course, be the opposite of yours.

This threatening approach may work for compliance audits, but that doesn't make it right. In fact, one of the main reasons that organizations are leery of the audit process is overeager auditors telling management what they must do to follow their interpretation of what the standard states. This approach severs the link to value-added reporting and ignores what is in the best interests of the organization. If the results cannot be sold on their own merit, then something is wrong.

Checklist for a Finding Statement

Statements that identify systematic problems (versus isolated errors) and show cause-and-effect relationships are the most effective in promoting improvement of the system. We recommend using finding statements where the audit purpose, scope, and organizational culture allow it.

A checklist for putting together a finding statement follows:

1. Collect the facts and ensure that they are clearly stated.
2. Identify the standard, procedure, customer requirement, organizational objective, goal, etc., that is not being satisfied.
3. Identify the pain to the organization (dollars, customer relationships, sales, or cost of quality).
4. State the system deficiency in the terms of the standard, goal, or the customer requirement in terms the user can understand.
5. When possible, relate the statement to the external customer (how could the external customer be affected?).
6. Ensure the statement is professional and unbiased.
7. Support the finding with evidence found in the audit.

SIDE BAR

During the design, development and implementation of a quality system nonconformity reports are very effective. In the early stages of a system deployment, most people only want to know what they need to do to complete their assignment (they cannot see the forest for the trees at this stage). As the system starts maturing, finding statements are more effective continuous improvement tools. An evolving corrective action system can be overloaded with identification of minor imperfections. Use of findings to identify systematic error will help management focus on the important issues.

Building blocks for writing a finding statement are found in Figure 2.2. The three building blocks are a starting point for writing a finding statement. A finding statement should include: (1) the control evaluated, (2) reason for problem found, and (3) the pain (potential or actual monetary effect) to the organization.

Two examples using the building blocks are:

1. Failure to follow product classification procedures has contributed to additional returns, sorting, and customer complaints.
2. Lack of control for off-shift deliveries has resulted in excessive rework.

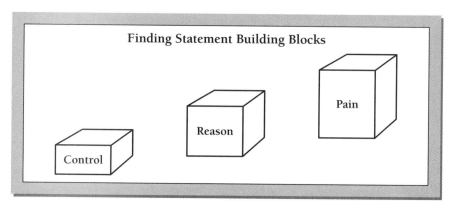

Figure 2.2. Finding statement building blocks.

Formatting and Organizing Reports

Now that the data analysis is finished and the findings are stated, it is time to prepare the report. If you are required to use a standardized format in your industry, do not be offended that you cannot add your own personal style. As a general rule, it is easier for auditors and management when a standard format is used. It is easier for the auditor because she does not have to spend time developing a new layout with each audit, and it is easier for management because they know where to find the "important stuff" in the report. Consider including the following elements in your audit report:

1. Title Page: contains the name of the organization, the address, the date of the audit, and the audit team members' names with their credentials.
2. Purpose: why the audit is being conducted.
3. Scope: the functions to be included in the audit.
4. Audit Standard: the quality system standard to be used in the audit.
5. Definitions: define terms such as *finding* and *nonconformance* so that people will know what they are reading. If the terms are known by the auditee or defined in a document or cover letter, this section would be optional.
6. Summary of Results: overall statement concerning the status of area audited.
7. Positive Practices or Noteworthy Achievements: an observation of an activity that is being performed in an outstanding manner

and should be shared with other areas, functions, departments, facilities, and locations.

8. Finding: the system concerns to be addressed by the auditee.

9. Nonconformities: a list of the symptoms found during the course of the audit that relate to a particular finding.

10. Additional Comments: any additional comments that might be helpful to the auditee.

This is a fairly simple format, but it is effective because there is no "excess baggage." Anything else (such as an overall summary) can be contained in the cover letter, which summarizes the key points for discussion in the exit meeting. You may think that this is an oversimplified approach, but keep in mind that the purpose of the report is to provide management with a clear statement of system concerns that must be corrected. The client should get a copy of the report exactly as provided to the auditee. The simpler the report layout, the easier it is to remain focused on the purpose of the report. Both the auditee and the client appreciate this approach because the facts are presented in a straightforward manner.

For a report to be effective, there should not be any distracters. The reporting of problems should be clear and correct. Each and every problem should be crystal clear and to the point. The information reported should be correct in terms of both the facts collected and the grammar used in the report. A misspelling is a distracter and takes power away from the report. A misplaced fact will erode your creditability.

If your organization uses nonconformance report (NCR) forms to report the results of an evaluation, toss them out. Our experience is that when people use NCR forms they tend to want to only focus on the isolated errors, not the system issues. Redesign the forms to report findings.

Summary

All management interests are linked to Cost-Opportunity-Risk (COR). When audit results are linked to COR they will receive a higher priority and management will see the benefits. The benefits are:

Reduced *cost* for providing the product or service.

Indentification of *opportunities* for new markets and new products or services.

Avoid *risk* to the wealth of the organization.

Auditors identify problems when (1) the system is not adequate to meet higher level standards (regulatory, ISO 9001, QS 9000), (2) people are not following the designed system, and (3) the system does not work. The three reasons for problems should be matched with COR to analyze the audit results in a Reason-Pain (R/P) Matrix. The final analysis is brought together using the finding statement building blocks.

Chapter 3

Deciding What to Do About It

We did not originally intend for this to be a book on problem solving. Yet, corrective action, or rather the lack of it, is where most organizations lose all the potential benefit of the audit process. We know that too many problems identified in audits are not resolved, but are identified as recurring problems in subsequent audits. Because we have seen corrective action failures (repeat problems) so many times, we want to review the problem-solving process in order to help you decide how to overcome your problem-solving success deficiency. This chapter will define a process to help you to decide what to do about the audit findings now that the audit is over.

We do not know many people who think audits are fun. Just the opposite. There are people who not only have the usual negative feelings about being audited, they also have a deep-seated dread of the entire experience. Whether or not you are one of those people, the following may seem familiar.

> The auditors have completed their report, conducted the exit meeting, and gone on their way. They have left you with the report, a stack of CARs, and a headache. There has been so much progress over the last several months, so many obstacles overcome, and now these auditors arrive to effortlessly identify, to be politically correct, "weaknesses" in the system that must be

addressed. Before the audit, you all thought you could see the light at the end of the tunnel, but now you are not even sure you can see the tunnel. There seems to be so much more to do now than ever before.

This scene, or one very much like it, has been described so many times that we began calling it "post-audit shock syndrome." The only successful way to cope with this malady is to have an effective method of establishing and maintaining control of the corrective action process. The temptation is for you, the manager, to begin making assignments for each of the various corrective action requests. However, your corrective action process has been successful only in that there was evidence to demonstrate that you were addressing existing concerns, but in many cases the problems returned. That means that the corrective action process itself is not effective or, at the very least, is deficient. For this situation to change, it is time to make a decision about your problem-solving process.

Paradise Lost

It is very possible that your problem-solving process, like many others, is based on the plan-do-check-act (PDCA) cycle. In his book *Out of the Crisis,* W. Edwards Deming describes this cycle as a procedure for improvement and "finding a special cause detected by a statistical signal."[5] This cycle, referred to by Deming as the Shewhart cycle, became known as a complete and comprehensive tool for management planning and improvement. This cycle remains one of the cornerstones for any company to find its way "out of the crisis." Unfortunately, what should be helping us find our way to paradise has become the path to perdition because what is being taught today has been diluted to just the four words without an adequate explanation of the actions necessary in each step of the cycle. Even when there is some explanation of the individual steps in the cycle, there is not enough emphasis on nor practice in the application of the PDCA cycle.

The PDCA cycle has been taught as a very simple, yet powerful problem-solving approach. It is unfortunate that the PDCA cycle has always been drawn as shown in Figure 3.1. Each of the individual phases of the cycle appear to be of equal proportion and, therefore, the attention given to each is roughly the same, at best. It has been taught this way as a mnemonic device so that managers may more easily remember and apply the concepts that lead to improvement. However, managers, being managers, understand and stress the simple, but fail to either see or to understand the PDCA cycle's complexity. In spite of this obvious shortcoming, managers are not entirely to blame for the abuse of this problem-solving tool. There are many training programs that tend to defeat the purpose of the PDCA cycle by treating the individual elements as though they are of equal importance, which they are not.

We have seen countless examples of organizations claiming to use the PDCA cycle as their primary problem-solving tool as well as their primary method of continuous improvement. Many are doing so because it is the simplest problem-solving methodology known to them, but they still cannot demonstrate its effectiveness. It is, obviously, the apparent simplicity that holds the attraction. PDCA appears so simple that many trainers and even consultants stress the lack of a requirement to keep records because "it just slows you down." These "experts" seem to have forgotten that this cycle had its origins in a book written by Walter A. Shewhart entitled *Statistical Method from the Viewpoint of Quality Control*.[6] They only say: "Just follow those four simple steps." As a result, many of the would-be problem solvers they have trained will "Plan," or investigate, only long enough for them to recognize that they know what to do because they have solved this problem at least a half-dozen times. Often, the "Plan" phase is ignored or shortened to the point that some of their people just jump feet first into "Do." Then they wonder what happened when they have to fix that same problem over and over again. This was never the way the PDCA cycle was intended to be implemented, and it is for this reason that we place such emphasis on the "Plan" phase of the cycle in the structured process described in "Defining the Process," on page 50.

PDCA Just Ain't That Simple

Managers recognize the need for training, but then tell trainers that they cannot take too much time. The trainers, not being independently wealthy, give what is asked for. So the lack of success in the PDCA cycle is not the fault of the cycle, but its improper application as a result of the shortcut methods in which its use is taught. If this business management improvement cycle is taught and implemented effectively, there should be no practical problems in achieving the desired improvement. Yet, even though the PDCA cycle is taught as a basic element of quality systems improvement and its importance as a management tool may be emphasized, it is rare that its application is really understood. Consider, for

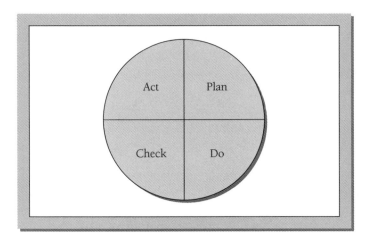

Figure 3.1. PDCA cycle.

example, Brian Joiner's comments regarding PDCA. In his book, *Fourth Generation Management,* he wrote:

> The basic notion of the PDCA cycle is so simple that when I first heard it I felt I understood it in five minutes. Now, more than a decade later, I think I might understand it some day.[7]

The PDCA cycle seems so simple that the concepts and techniques required for success in our complex business systems are frequently either cut short or ignored. This is evidenced by the fact that so many corrective actions do not prevent recurrence of problems. It is obvious that the simple method of representing this complex management planning process, as in Figure 3.1, has been effective. Unfortunately, it is also often taught in that same manner, omitting the techniques required to make it effective. In too many of the training materials we have reviewed, there is not even a discussion about the actions to be considered for each of the four "simple" steps. While we will agree that there is nothing wrong with conveying a complex idea or practice in a simple manner, the method of presentation should be changed when practice begins to more accurately represent the devotion to a picture rather than the principles intended.

Revising the Picture

Now, we are not saying that there is anything wrong with the PDCA cycle, nor that you are wrong to employ it. We would prefer, however, that you

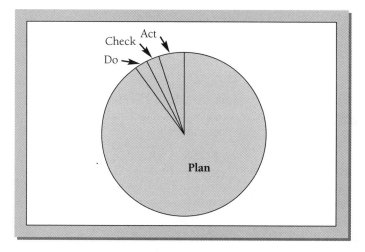

Figure 3.2. Time-Based PDCA.

understood the complexity of actions to be considered when employing this "simple" business management planning concept. For that reason, when we illustrate the relationship of the elements of the PDCA cycle proportionately as they should be drawn, the proportions are much more like those shown in Figure 3.2. In this figure, the "Plan" phase has approximately a nine-to-one activity ratio to the other elements of the cycle. That is to say that when you are engaged in any problem-solving or improvement activities, 90 percent of your activity should be devoted to PLANning-related activities. The remaining 10 percent should be devoted to the "Do-Check-Act" phases of the cycle.

We realize that this may appear to be heresy, but the fact of the matter is that by the time you complete the "Plan" phase, a large part of your work should be finished. The "Do" phase is one of very short duration. In effect, the actions decided upon during the "Plan" phase are executed for a very short period of time as a test, not as the termination of the exercise. This test lasts just as long as necessary to gather the data required to determine the effectiveness of the "Plan." The "Check" phase is only of sufficient duration to analyze the data gathered to verify the effectiveness of the "Plan" executed during the "Do" phase. The "Check" phase is also the time for making a decision as to whether or not the data gathered in the short execution of the "Plan" proves that this action will achieve the desired result. In the last phase of the cycle, you "Act" on your decision to implement the corrective action (or improvement) or to reevaluate the "Plan" for improved performance. It is in this "Act" phase that action is implemented. In other words, you have determined the actions necessary to correct the root cause, but you have also evaluated the effectiveness of the corrective action to prevent the occurrence of other potential nonconformities.

Connections

We have yet to meet a manager who implemented a corrective action process just to have something else to do. Yet, there seems to be no link between an organization's business objectives and a corrective action team's problem-solving goals. This may explain the lack of emphasis on the corrective action team's maintaining records of actions and results. It is almost as though a team's process improvement actions bear no relationship to the organization's success.

Some trainers may argue that the team minutes will contain all the information needed to provide that link. This *might* be true if the team members were thoroughly trained and disciplined enough to use team techniques. However, only one trainer in ten has demonstrated practical knowledge of effective team techniques and understood the importance of defining and documenting the problem to be solved. Many trainers actually teach trial-and-error problem-solving under the guise of PDCA. Which brings us back to our starting point of fixing the problem so it doesn't happen again.

It is true that many problems are solved quite effectively every day without consulting an elaborate database. Recognizing this as a fact, however, does not mean that all the people in your organization will be successful problem solvers just because we tell them about PDCA. You and your people must be committed to the organization's goals and objectives, understand your customer's needs, and have the means to monitor and improve your processes. We would like you to remind you that many of the people that you need to be involved in the problem-solving process:

- Are not always the process experts
- Are not always experienced in problem-solving techniques
- May not understand the complexities of the system you are trying to improve
- May believe all this "program of the month" activity will end soon
- May not understand the importance of the concern in question
- May see the concern as your priority, not theirs

These points seem only to represent the negative side. On the positive side, people are eager to be involved and are more than willing to improve their work performance. The decision you must make is whether or not to initiate actions that commit you to implementing a process of corrective and preventive actions involving all your people. If you do, then you may also need to make a change in your internal communications system. While you may have defined your business goals in terms that are meaningful to your organization and your customers, have these goals been communicated to the people within your organization? Have you provided them with the means to achieve those goals? Have they been provided with regular performance updates? If so, great! But there is one other thing you need to do. You need to ensure that the corrective action goals you or your staff set are linked to your business goals. If they are not, then why are they important to your organization or your customers?

The Problem with Data

Your present method of measuring performance may tell you that you are doing well. Sales are up, inventory is in control, quality is good, and your profits are above average for your industry, but your customers are still not happy. How can all these indicators be positive and there still be so many problems? Your business-results measures may tell you that you are doing well, but are you effectively measuring your business processes? The measures you have implemented may be allowing you to be complacent (self-contented) about the efficiency of your true business process performance.

If you only measure the end result, you may be surprised to find that it is what you have *not* measured that holds the key for you to improve. You may believe this is impossible, but unless you know the variation in your business processes, you cannot be sure. The problem may not be with the data you have but with the data you *do not* have. To improve your business management system's performance, you must first improve the basis for making your business decisions.

The problem with the data you use each day to make business decisions is that you may be basing your actions on facts that are only as good as you want them to be. For example, one company tracked delivery performance as a measure of customer satisfaction. Their internal measures indicated they had achieved a 95 percent on-time delivery performance level. They were not pleased to learn that their customers gave them a 60 percent rating on delivery. The reason was that when an order was taken, the delivery date was frequently extended because the customer's request could not be met. Delivery performance was measured against the extended date, not the customer's original request. The method of measuring performance was changed and the company worked hard to achieve a performance rating of 82 percent on-time delivery. When the company measured what was important to the customer, their customer satisfaction rating went up.

Your business decisions should be based on accurate, reproducible data that is representative of the system's performance. You cannot be sure unless you have verified that you are receiving reliable data for the picture of your business performance. If you are willing to face up to "the good, the bad, and the ugly" realities of your business system, then there may be hope for continued improvement of your corrective action process.

Defining the Process

We redrew the diagram in Figure 3.2 to illustrate the importance of planning, but we did not provide any of the important stuff that we believe is necessary for improved corrective action performance. The following is a list of each phase of the PDCA cycle with the corresponding steps of the corrective action process, which are described later in this chapter as well as in the next chapter:

Plan:

1. Evaluate the relationship of concern to organizational goals.
2. Select a team to investigate the concern.
3. Determine necessary remedial actions.
4. Gather and analyze data.
5. Define the problem.
6. Determine root cause.
7. Determine alternatives to test.
8. Define measures for effectiveness.
9. Determine and verify corrective and preventive actions.

Do:

10. Test corrective and preventive action alternatives.

Check:

11. Collect and monitor performance data.

Act:

12. Evaluate results.

13. Standardize improvement actions.

14. Ensure application in similar process and/or products.

Simple, right? Of course, it is when you have all the right elements in place. For instance:

- Business goals have been communicated to all personnel.
- Customer expectations are known and understood.
- Process performance data is available to all personnel.
- All personnel have been trained in team techniques.
- All personnel have been trained in basic SPC techniques.
- All personnel have been trained in basic problem-solving techniques.
- All personnel understand the business goal/improvement goal link.

It should be apparent that we must understand the current level of performance before we can initiate improvement actions. But must everyone have all this training before we begin trying to improve the process? While it would be ideal to train everyone first, it would hardly be practical to do so. There is a business to operate, after all. So, how do you begin this improvement stuff?

The Importance of Being Earnest

Setting your business goals is an annual part of your planning process. These goals are what you have set out to achieve in the coming year in order to support your long-term plan. Depending on the nature of your industry, these goals may be affected monthly or even weekly by changes in the marketplace. Are you to change your goals weekly or are you to adjust the actions required to achieve the goals?

Changing goals daily or weekly is as dangerous as a diabetic's changing insulin dosage just to compensate for sugar intake. Insulin is a medication that must be controlled at a constant rate, not adjusted to compensate for one's dietary "mistakes." A diabetic's goal is not a daily goal, but one that is lifelong. Sugar intake must be restricted at three years of age so one may live to enjoy 63. The same is true with your business goals.

Once set as the direction for your organization, day-to-day actions and decisions must be coordinated consistently to achieve those goals. Like the diabetic, whose daily routine must be balanced with the proper dietary and insulin intake, your business systems must be balanced, coordinated, and consistent. Also, like the diabetic, your business alternative is to experience a self-limiting, unhealthy, and, in all probability, short existence.

Tracking Performance

Once goals are set, key process measures should be identified. These key measures are derived from those processes that directly affect the successful achievement of those goals. Several different measures may be required for each goal. For example, material utilization may be measured by comparing raw materials received to product shipped. But what happens between the time materials are received and the product is shipped? How much scrap and rework is generated? Are production schedules maintained? Is the shipment schedule maintained only because the rework department achieves a 99.5 percent recovery? If so, there are opportunities for improvement.

Depending on the size of your organization, the complexity of the product or service, the volume of parts produced, etc., you may need to monitor performance daily to achieve consistent results. As trends in the performance of key processes are developed, they will guide you in making the proper decisions regarding improvement actions. This does not necessarily mean that you have to construct an expensive auxiliary reporting system. You may only need to restructure a few reports from information that is already being generated to provide the data necessary for monitoring process performance. Whatever reporting system you use, it should be comprehensive enough to provide the data needed to evaluate the key process performance issues. At the same time, it should not require a separate staff to maintain. The intent is to provide up-to-date performance information to those responsible for process improvement, not to add a new department.

Prepare for Improvement

Training
Yes, we know you have a business to run. You cannot afford to have your key people off the line for days at a time. We agree. The problem with

training has always been that it requires one day per session away from the operation, so when training is going on, work has to stop. Training does not have to be done this way just because it has been done that way in the past. There are ways to train small groups or teams effectively at times that are convenient for your operation with minimal loss of production. As you evaluate the most effective training schedule to meet your needs, try to arrange training sessions with a combination of line and staff personnel. During the communication age several alternate training mediums and techniques have emerged. Depending on the need, timing, and learning objectives, there is a training program to fit almost every budget. When asked if instructor-lead training was more effective than web-based training, a well-known instructional designer said: "Studies indicate that one is not more effective than the other." A poorly designed training class in any medium is second-rate.

Improvement Teams

In the beginning, a cross-functional team should be formed to identify key measures and opportunities. Once the key measures have been identified, be consistent in the comparison methods. Initially, the teams will make a few mistakes because they are learning to apply new techniques. It is for this reason that the teams should use a structured process in their approach to this improvement process. The key process measures, which are linked to the business performance goals, should be reported daily and summarized on a weekly and monthly basis. The teams may then use this data as a basis for monitoring their performance.

The management team should periodically take time to review performance and compare to the set goals. After all, you did determine that there were specific business goals to be achieved. If you are to be successful, every system, every department, every process must be aligned with those goals. If performance toward the goal is not as expected, then an adjustment may be made, not in the goal, but in the resources applied in that area to re-evaluate and support the team addressing that issue.

If you are to have a single set of goals and one method of reporting performance, then it makes sense to adopt one problem-solving methodology. Now, we have said before that PDCA is a management planning tool that has its foundations based in statistical methods, so the analysis of data and record keeping are important. We also know that you are interested in consistent performance over time in not only correcting problems, but also preventing recurrence of problems. So, we will continue to emphasize the need for teams to keep records of their progress in each step because there are interactions in your systems, you are implementing a new corrective action process, and your teams are relatively inexperienced in employing the techniques. You will find that records are beneficial because:

- Teams will be able to re-evaluate their actions more effectively.
- Improved performance can be proven to customers (and auditors).
- Team's sponsor can verify that actions are based on business goals.
- Teams can demonstrate that actions are based on process data.

We have offered a more structured method of problem solving for consideration because we have seen that there are too few effective corrective actions being taken in response to customer complaints with too little data to verify results, and too many problems being repeated. It is exactly this repeated failure that we want you to avoid whether you are addressing internal issues, customer concerns, or audit corrective actions. Developing and implementing your corrective action process as we have described provides:

- Improved problem definition.
- Better documentation of actions implemented.
- Improved team success.
- Improved corrective action performance.

A very important element in the implementation process is consistency in the application of a structured process and the recording of results. Taking shortcuts will serve only to create variation in the process. Be patient, use the same process every time, and you will be successful.

Preventive Actions

Now, we agree that consistency is important when investigating and implementing corrective action, but with regard to preventive action, you may want to ask:

- What is it?
- When does it begin?
- How is it done?
- Is this a separate process?
- Why can I not get straight answers?

There is one answer to these questions which is simple and straightforward. The answer is as follows:

- It is the same thing, and
- is done at the same time,
- in the same way,
- using the same process, but
- the corrective/preventive action relationship is not understood.

Take a minute to ask yourself this question, "When did this preventive action thing first become a confusing issue?" The timing strangely coincides with the 1994 revision of ISO 9001. But please do not place blame on the International Organization for Standardization. Prior to this revision, there was, and still is, a legitimate problem recognized by auditors.

The Problem: too often, real improvement actions are not taken and not effective.

The Solution: emphasize preventive action in the 1994 revision.

This change was to send a simple message that effective improvement actions are the expectation of the standard. It was a good plan that would have worked. If not for auditors, that is.

The best method of demonstrating compliance with the corrective and preventive action requirement is to have one documented process that:

- Emphasizes the identification of the root cause of a defined problem
- Prevents the recurrence of problems
- Prevents the occurrence of potential problems

That is, the process not only identifies the root cause of the defined problem, but also identifies potential sources of problems and prevents their occurrence as the defined problem is resolved. Again, be consistent in the application of this process in all areas of your system, and you will be successful when you plan for and implement corrective action.

An Example of Corrective Action

We have provided you with a lot of detail about the problem-solving process. We will now provide you with an illustration of the corrective action process at work. This example has two characters: Mr. Homeowner (you), who has little experience with our corrective action process, and Mr. Electrician, who is very experienced in this corrective action process. These two characters are to investigate a simple everyday problem like a lamp that does nothing when it is turned on.

The lamp by your favorite chair does not light up when you turn the switch. You re-arranged the furniture a few days ago, but cannot remember using the lamp since then. You check the usual simple things like the cord, the plug, and the bulb. When you examine the bulb, you find that it is blown. So, you conclude that the root cause of the lamp failure is a blown bulb caused by rough handling during the re-arranging. Your solution for the light that doesn't work is to change the bulb. You do and it does. However, you notice a short time later that the lamp is not working again. So, you change the bulb again only to repeat the same process within a relatively short period. Being the intelligent person you are, you say: "Hey, I think something's wrong with this lamp."

Now you get serious and bring in 70 pounds of tools to work on this three-pound lamp. You unplug the lamp and remove the lampshade to take a closer look at the socket. The contacts look good, and since you do not want to let the tools go to waste, you remove the socket to examine the wiring connections. You find that one of the screws seems to be a bit loose and one of the wires is all but free of the connection. Examining the cord, you find a mark on the insulation that indicates it has been tugged pretty hard from near the base of the lamp. This is more evidence of the rough treatment which you suspected caused the original problem. Just to be sure, you summarize the sequence of events:

- Furniture moved
- Blown bulbs
- Loose connection found in the socket
- Insulation on the cord is also marked
- Root cause: damaged wire connection during the move
- Tightened wire connection

Conclusion: the lamp is repaired.

You are useful. Satisfaction reigns. Life is good.

Until that same lamp blows another bulb.

The analysis of root cause in this example is similar to the preliminary analysis during the development of the action plan (discussed in the next chapter.) All the information gathered may be too limited to prevent recurrence. It is for this reason that alternative actions should be examined and tested. Now let's go back to the example and find out what happens when reinforcements (skilled resources) are introduced:

When you find out that the lamp has another blown bulb, you take the lamp to your work area and check the socket again. Since everything is in order, you decide to call your neighbor, who just happens to be an electrician. But the questions he asks are not at all what you expect. Your neighbor, Mr. Electrician, asks you:

- Have you experienced any problems with any other appliances?
- Is there a pattern in the length of time the bulbs last before you find them blown?
- Were all the bulbs from the same lot?
- Have you used these bulbs as replacements in any other lamps?
- What other electrical devices do you use in that room?
- How old is the house?
- Who was the electrical contractor?

Your understandable, though unhelpful, response is: "Uh . . . what? How should I know?"

Mr. Electrician then proceeds with a lengthy and almost unintelligible explanation about house wiring and circuits that is more that you ever really wanted to know. You simply say: "Yeah, right. Can we fix it?" He just gives you a nod and goes, not where you expected, which is to the room where the lamp is located, but to the electrical panel in the garage.

He explains as he goes that the blown bulbs are not the problem, but a symptom of the problem. The lamp is only a single element in the electrical system of the house which is where the problem seems to be.

This response should not be too surprising. In fact, this response should not be very different from the problems encountered in any working environment. What is different about Mr. Electrician's response is only that he has defined the problem from a different perspective. He has evaluated the problem from a consideration of the entire electrical system using the symptoms and the other information provided to determine the alternatives to test. As we said before, the symptom is not the problem to be solved. The symptom should be only the guide we use to gather information about the system, as we will see as we continue with the example.

As Mr. Electrician opens the panel, he explains, "The sequence of the symptoms you described indicates to me that the problem did not occur until the lamp was moved. That change did not mean that the system itself had changed, but your use of it had. In other words, a chance event—your moving the lamp—initiated the event itself, and may have prevented you from having more serious problems later. What I am looking for now is the same thing you were looking for originally, which is a loose wire. I am just looking in the most likely place that will give me the most information about the electrical system."

If you refer to the list (page 61) where we correlated the PDCA cycle to our corrective action process, you will find that Mr. Electrician is gathering additional information to analyze and define the problem. Those questions he asked, though meaningless to you, were the starting point of his investigation. As you will find out as you learn more about the process, the questions to be asked are very important. Problem-solving teams should be encouraged to ask and entertain questions. If the information is not available, go to the source and find it. The answers, however, take time and experience. Mr. Electrician's explanation is a good example:

"What you had defined as the root cause may have been logical, but it is just the same as at work. People doing the initial investigation are working with limited information when defining the problem. They must realize the limitations of the data they use to develop the action plans and allow for additional time for a more thorough analysis. In this case, the problem is not that complex, but I still tend to use the same steps to solve problems.

"What I see here caused the symptoms to appear in the first place, but it is still not the problem. This loose wire needs to be tightened down, but the screw is stripped. I could move the wire to a different slot, but it is too short. If I tighten it to the point just before it slips, it might hold, but that will not prevent a future problem. All someone would have to do is to turn this screw just a little, and the wire would be loose again. I will rethread it and put in a new screw to prevent that from happening again, but I will have to go back inside and examine your receptacles to be sure that any future problems are not likely to occur."

Mr. Electrician is doing exactly what should be done when taking corrective and preventive actions. He has used the information initially provided to begin his investigations. He proceeded to gather more information about the system to implement corrective actions. However, as he does so, he also identifies the possible preventive actions necessary to eliminate the possibility of potential problems. He will continue to examine the system until he is certain that he has correctly identified the preventive actions necessary and then implement them. This process requires patience on the part of the investigators and implementers. It requires a complete and thorough analysis of the system, but you should avoid the temptation to over analyze. Take the King of Hearts' advice: "Begin at the beginning, and when you come to the end, stop." Just like Mr. Electrician.

"I have isolated the circuit that is involved. I also found that there have been some modifications made to your electrical system that are not noted in the listing on your panel. I replaced the old legend with a new one that lists each of the existing circuits. I have also verified from an examination of your panel and the receptacles in each room that the six receptacles along these walls are the only ones affected by the problem, which was neither the lamp, nor the screw, but an alternative wiring method that is not a recommended practice for home wiring systems. That is the good news. The bad news is that the most cost-effective alternative for a solution that I can offer for the present is to replace each receptacle in this room. The best solution for the problem is to replace the entire circuit, but that will cost quite a bit. Properly wiring the new receptacles will effectively prevent future problems and will only cost about $20.

"Given what we found, you could have lost much more than a few light bulbs. I am going to add a jumper in each box and replace the six receptacles to avoid problems in the future. Unless someone changes out a receptacle and counteracts what I have done, there should not be any more problems. Just to be sure, I will mark the breakers and make a notation in the panel to exercise caution when working with that circuit. Still, in spite of these precautions, you should consider changing out that circuit. In the long run, it will be the safest bet to prevent someone from making a simple change that brings everything back to the starting point. It's your house and your decision to make."

Mr. Electrician has been very thorough in his investigation of the problem and the possible alternatives. He has kept records of the modifications he has made to the system and he has informed you of his reasons for making each one. He has even provided you with information regarding the "opportunities" for improvement or the consequences if these modifications to the electrical system are not implemented. He has also demonstrated that four different "solutions" did not address the symptoms' root cause:

- Changing light bulbs
- Repairing the lamp
- Replacing the screw
- Replacing and properly wiring the receptacles

In fact, he has not yet corrected the root cause—the circuit. He has, however, implemented every alternative while recommending the best solution. Mr. Homeowner now has to make the decision whether or not to implement the solution recommended by the expert. The final decision is the ever-present conflict between cost-effectiveness and risk. In order to be sure you understand the problem-solving steps in this example, we restated what has taken place in Table 3.1.

In more complex problems, the corrective action process takes longer, but the steps involved are the same. Being thorough while gathering data and keeping records for the future are both very important, especially when you know the likelihood of your being on hand when the next problem occurs is very low.

The previous example illustrates that there may be several symptoms which seem to be causes for even simple problems. Stopping too soon, without evaluating relevant elements of the system, will not prevent the problem from recurring. Another point that may be taken from this example is that the effectiveness of the most thorough and exacting corrective and preventive action process can be negated by the lack of implementation of the solution recommended. In fact, there are several things that jeopardize the corrective action process:

- Not selecting the proper team members
- Not having the proper mix of skills on the team
- Failing to define the problem correctly
- Not using a logical process

We've progressed from looking at the forest to studying the trees—from setting organization (business) goals to effective problem solving. Now it is time to return to the forest perspective. You always want problem solving to be effective. However, if the problem being addressed does not aid the achievement of the business goals or address customer needs, then—effective or not—nothing has been accomplished for the organization. Stating the team's mission or objective in measurable terms will help you to ensure that the team's activities are in line with organizational/business goals.

Chapter 4

The Corrective and Preventive Action Process

Some people want to call any improvement process a corrective or preventive action program, while others say we should focus on the positive and talk about new opportunities for improvement. Real-world experiences lead us to believe that people don't start correcting or improving until they figure out that there will be some benefit to them or their organization for their efforts: the WIIFM ("What's in it for me?") theory. Sometimes they figure out for themselves that they have a problem (opportunity?), and other times someone else tells them (through audits, assessments, examinations).

Improvement actions may stem from a problem statement, whether the result of a recognized noncompliance or the realization that a new product design will probably cause excessive returns. So, in many cases, correcting is improving, preventing is improving, improving is correcting, and improving is preventing. In other words, things equal to the same thing are equal to each other. Correcting a problem presents an opportunity to improve, and initiating action to take advantage of an opportunity pre-supposes the existence of a problem for the organization or individual. Such action also indicates that potential concerns (that have yet to make themselves known) may be lurking in the shadows. In this book, we will use the term *corrective/preventive action* to describe the process, and the term *problem* as the input to the process.

Continuous Correcting Is Not Continuous Quality Improvement

Some training organizations teach that corrective action is continuous improvement. Corrective action is a part of continuous improvement but certainly does not represent an entire continuous quality improvement program. Continuous quality improvement has many aspects, elements, and ingredients. In order to ensure profitable continuous improvement activities, the following elements or attributes should be integrated into your organizational culture:

- A process to reduce variation that is integrated into the management philosophy
- A preventive style of management for doing all work right the first time
- A feedback system for customers and suppliers (both internal and external)
- A means for promoting and motivating people to participate

Although continuous improvement is not the focus of this book, we want you to understand that these attributes are important for continuous improvement activities to succeed. We also want to make it perfectly clear that just because you have a corrective action program does not mean that you have achieved continuous quality improvement. We also want to remind you that continuous quality improvement is not just about solving problems. While continuous quality improvement may begin with the investigation of a problem, or an identified concern which has the potential for becoming "a problem," there are always issues or opportunities for improvement which are raised through this process that will lead to further improvement. Continuous quality improvement is not a linear process, but a cyclical process for achieving optimal performance and customer satisfaction.

Corrective and Preventive Actions

Corrective/ Preventive Action, ISO Style
The ISO 9000 and ISO 10011 series standards provide a good framework for corrective and preventive action that will be used in this book. The 1994 issue of the ISO 9000 series standards added the word preventive action to the corrective action clause of the ISO 9001 and ISO 9002 standards.

The introduction of a separate sub-clause for "preventive action" led to an astonishing amount of discussion and confusion. However, like you, we are practitioners who believe the confusion can be remedied, and provide the following explanation to clarify this issue. We would like to clarify these terms by providing a slight variation to the ISO 9000:2000 definitions in order to provide some insight into the difference between them.

Corrective Action: an action taken to eliminate the cause(s) of existing nonconformities (problems) or any other undesirable situation in order to prevent recurrence.

Your house roof is more than 20 years old and has started to leak. You replace the roof and repair the ceiling in the master bedroom where the roof leaked.

Preventive Action: an action taken to eliminate the cause(s) of potential nonconformities (problems) or other undesirable situation in order to prevent occurrence.

You determine that your house roof is more than 20 years old and that 20 year shingles were installed. You replace the roof before it starts to leak.

These definitions state that you must eliminate causes to either prevent occurrence or prevent recurrence of potential problems (nonconformities). When done correctly, determining the cause (that is, the underlying or root cause) of a problem (nonconformity) and taking action to prevent it from happening again is not always easy. The reason is that, for our actions to be effective, we must have reliable information about our process and service or product performance and we must employ systems thinking (systems thinking is discussed in chapter 1).

In many cases, people within organizations may decide that they can get by with implementing a quick fix or remedy for a problem that does not address the underlying cause. People implement quick fixes either because the problem seems minor or as a "band-aid" to take some action while awaiting a final resolution. It is an interim action between the identification of the undesirable situation and implementing a corrective action. Quick fixes are common, so we need a term to define this type of action. We will call quick fixes *remedial* (or containment) actions.

Remedial (Containment) Action: an action taken to alleviate the symptoms of existing nonconformities or any other undesirable situation.

Your house roof is more than 20 years old and has started to leak. You patch the roof with roofing tar to stop the leak and replaster the ceiling in the master bedroom where the roof already leaked.

Remedial action may be taken as an intermediate step in the corrective action process. For example, you have defined a problem but you need to take steps to minimize its effects before you can identify the root cause and determine the best solution. In that case, you might initiate 100 percent sorting activities, or retesting, to avoid the possibility of questionable product reaching the next stage in the process or, worse, your customers. There may be times when you do not have enough data to be convinced that a problem is serious enough for you to initiate full-blown corrective action. At other times, you may rationalize that taking remedial action is acceptable because you do not have time to initiate full-blown corrective action for everything.

> **Caution:** The practice of taking remedial action should not be abused. Though we recognize the practice of taking remedial action, this should not be used as a license to avoid implementing corrective/preventive action on "the important stuff."

A good example of when remedial action may be appropriate happened the same week we were developing this chapter. A facility was audited by a third-party auditor who issued a nonconformity stating: "Some of the procedures are not referenced in the quality manual." This type of nonconformity statement is disappointing and demoralizing to the audited organization. Would you initiate a full-blown corrective action investigation to determine underlying causes, evaluate the process of developing quality manuals and putting all procedure numbers in the document, and possibly issuing new procedures for writing a quality manual? We hope not! What you should do is add the missing procedure reference to the manual at the next issue. This is remedial action: No underlying causes were investigated, and the system didn't change. It isn't worth consuming 160 hours of a person's time to investigate and implement a root-cause solution.

When you are addressing the root cause of a problem because of a known defect, you are implementing corrective (and not preventive) actions. When you are fixing the root cause of a potential problem as a result of analysis, you are implementing preventive (not corrective) actions. The input to remedial, corrective, and preventive actions are shown in Figure 4.1.

The process starts with the identification of the product or service problem (nonconforming product). An example of a problem may be that a product does not meet specifications, such as a report with errors, a rental car that was not properly cleaned to be customer ready, or merchandise that was damaged. Then problem detection is combined with deficiencies found from audits and customer complaints to form the inputs to correc-

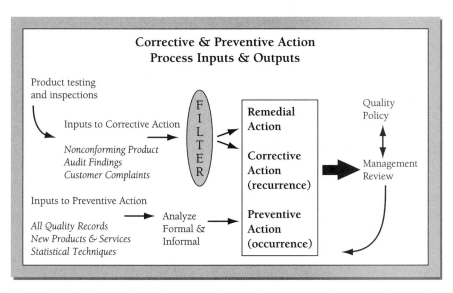

Figure 4.1. Corrective and preventive action process inputs and outputs.

tive action. All the inputs are existing problems identified with a product or service. The problems are then reviewed (filtered or screened) to determine what action to take. The choices are: (1) do nothing because it is an isolated error or a minor issue, (2) take remedial action, or (3) take corrective action. Thus corrective action is being reactive: reacting to every product, service, or quality system (from audits) failure.

The second input to the corrective/preventive action process is from the analysis of performance data. All records can be analyzed to reveal positive and negative trends or outcomes. The records analyzed should include all quality records such as nonconforming product or service (it's bad, it's wrong, it didn't work), audit results, and customer complaints. In many cases, statistical techniques (statistical process control charts, trend charts, histograms, Pareto charts, scatter diagrams, cause-and-effect diagrams, etc.) are used to analyze data and processes. Analyzing data will point out potential improvement areas so that action can be taken to prevent (pro-active) the occurrence of an "unplanned event." Other common pro-active initiatives include analyzing the results of customer surveys, conducting capability studies of processes, and failure mode and effects analysis (FMEA).

In fact, the FMEA may be the most frequently documented example of preventive action available. There are two kinds of FMEAs: design FMEAs and process FMEAs. Design FMEAs are applied during the design stages of product or service. Process FMEAs are applied to new or existing processes (a defined series of steps that lead to desired result). The purpose of both is to identify potential failure modes (problems with the design or process) and eliminate or at least, minimize their effects. The methodology employed is to evaluate the system—systems thinking—to ensure that all potential failure modes are considered, whether product or process related. Although all possible failure modes cannot be eliminated, controls can be implemented to minimize or eliminate their effects.

Intuitive Analysis

We have included the word informal in the corrective/preventive model because the identification of the need to practice preventive action is not always the result of a formal analysis. There are informal and intuitive inputs (for example, you believe performance could be better than it is now). In many ways, the informal intuitive analysis (what many of us do every day in our jobs) is superior to formal analysis because the human brain can consider a vast number of variables at one time and sort out irrelevant information. The problem with relying solely in intuitive analysis is that it is inconsistent—we don't always have enough relevant data for our brains to process. The problem with relying solely on formal (computerized) analysis is that the assumptions or model may have changed and program changes are lagging.

We recognize there are times that facts, or data, are not the problem. It is often the case that it is not the facts, but our interpretation of the facts that is the problem. In our own experience, we have found that the "facts" indicate that a specific action is appropriate, but we "know" (our intuition has "kicked in") that the action indicated by the facts is incorrect. In that case, we have two options: we can either stop until we can obtain more data, or we can act. Unfortunately, the reality is that we either do not always have the luxury of time or we do not always take the time to analyze a situation thoroughly. Sometimes people do not always have sufficient information on hand for a good intuitive analysis.

Intuitive analysis is a very valuable (if not the most value-added) input into the preventive action process. It would not surprise us to learn that many preventive action projects are initiated when someone within the organization is able to foresee a potential problem (or opportunity) when the facts did not indicate the possibility of such an occurrence. You don't need to be a psychic or clairvoyant to provide input to the improvement process, it comes from being a good manager, supervisor, or associate. You are collecting information and interpreting it rather than waiting for a computer to do it for you.

Corrective Action and Preventive Action Defined

If you take action to eliminate the cause of a problem as a result of a reported product or service problem (nonconformity), customer complaint, or quality system audit, you are practicing corrective action (reactive). If you take action to eliminate the cause of a problem as a result of analyzing data, you are practicing preventive action (pro-active). This is oversimplified, but it provides a framework for us to begin our discussion.

Corrective versus Preventive Action Quagmire

There have been heated discussions over e-mail circuits, on the telephone, in conferences, and at local pubs about classifying the actions to cure problems as either dispositioning, taking remedial action (not addressing the underlying cause), corrective action, and preventive action. Since solving problems can be complicated, issues are not always black and white. Attempts to classify actions should not overshadow the value-added process of improvement.

The difference between action taken in response to a reported problem and actions initiated in recognition of a given set of performance conditions, is the difference between corrective action and preventive action. Yet, they are part of one set of activities when you "fix it" and make sure "it" does not happen again. Here is an example.

> **Corrective Action:** Rachel was late for work yesterday because she lost her car keys. Now she has an extra set of keys in the garage under the oil can.

> **Preventive Action:** Paul had an extra set car keys made that he hid in the garage under the flowerpot in case he misplaces his original keys and needs to go someplace quickly (such as to work).

The examples seem straightforward, but, then again, they may not be. Why was Paul so wise to get an extra set of keys?

1. Maybe he was late to work four times last year due to misplaced keys and finally realized this was a recurring problem that he could remedy.

2. Maybe his wife is always borrowing his keys and he is tired of looking for her when he needs to use the car.

3. Maybe he realized that if he ever misplaced his keys in the morning that he could be late for work and his pay would be docked or he could get fired.

4. Maybe Paul noticed that a fellow employee was late several times and gave the excuse that he misplaced his keys.

5. Maybe Paul is competing for a promotion with someone who comes in late to work all the time.

If we were to ask people to classify Paul's actions as either corrective or preventive we would get many different answers. Take another look at reason number 1: since Paul was late for work in the past, maybe he is practicing corrective action (reacting) instead of preventive action (being proactive)? Now re-examine reason number 2: since Paul's wife borrows the keys and doesn't return them, is Paul actually reacting to a problem? Arguments can be developed to support several points of view. That's the first part of the quagmire.

The second part of the quagmire is whether Rachel's or Paul's actions address the underlying cause. We could argue that neither Rachel or Paul are addressing the underlying cause and, therefore, they are both practicing remedial action, not corrective or preventive action. Maybe Rachel should change her habits to always store her keys in a certain place. Maybe Rachel should see a hypnotist to address her habits. Maybe Paul should wear his keys around his neck so that they will always be on his person. Maybe, since Paul's wife won't change her habit of using his keys, he should eliminate the cause and divorce her. We could go on and on. The point is that we must avoid this quagmire.

When you are reacting to a specific defect, nonconformity, finding, or customer complaint, you are initiating the corrective action process. When you are analyzing data (defects, nonconformities, surveys, complaints, corrective actions, and so on) to determine potential concerns to be addressed, you are taking preventive action. Of course, you will also analyze process data to determine root cause as a step in this process.

Then, out of the blue, someone will suggest (with good intentions) that inspection is preventive action, since no defect initiated the inspection. This statement makes many of us shudder, since we know that inspection is an appraisal cost and is a result of the lack of prevention. This is yet another argument to add to the quagmire.

Fundamental Corrective/Preventive Action Steps

What is important is that you have a process that will:

- Find important problems (opportunities).
- Find the cause(s).
- Find a solution for the cause(s).
- Fix the problem (eliminate the cause).

- Make sure it doesn't happen again.
- Keep records.

Every organization should define how it is to go about correcting and preventing problems. However, you will find as you review this list that your organization does not need two separate processes (one for corrective action and one for preventive action). As we progress from chapter to chapter we will use an established corrective/preventive action system as our model.

Real-Life Corrective/Preventive Action Examples

Fiber Drum Example

Customer Complaint 40411: customer ABC complained that product is in different-sized fiber drums.

Background: supplier uses re-conditioned drums to ship new production.

Action: put a special instruction message in the customer file to use only new drums when filling customer ABC's orders.

Customer Complaint 40411 closed April 21.

The action to address this customer complaint falls in the remedial category since there was no attempt to eliminate the underlying cause. The same company, however, issued the following corrective action request months later.

Corrective Action Request 41101: the analysis of customer complaints shows that 50 percent of the product packaging complaints involve the use of reconditioned drums.

Background: supplier uses 20 percent reconditioned drums to reduce packaging costs.

Action: it was determined that the cost of handling the complaints and potential loss of customer satisfaction outweighed the savings derived from using reconditioned drums. From now on only new drums will be used in the manufacturing plant.

Result: product packaging complaints dropped by 50 percent.

Corrective Action Request 41101 closed on December 15.

The action to address the negative trend in packaging complaints would be in the preventive action category since data were analyzed to detect areas for preventing undesirable situations. You could argue that this is actually corrective action since the supplier was reacting to customer complaints. How you classify an action may depend on timing and your approach to a problem. Here, the individual complaints could be easily handled with special instructions for each customer order. It was not until the data were analyzed that the supplier realized the significance of the problem (several complaints with a common cause).

Vernier Calipers Example[8]

Corrective Action Request #304: April 5

Process Deviation: an audit revealed that a mill operator was using vernier calipers with no calibration sticker.

Corrective Action Taken: mill operator was interviewed by the team leader. Operator stated that the machinists often used an old pair of calipers for rough-cutting because the metal chips foul the gears of their precision calipers and they wind up having to replace the expensive ($150) calipers every few months. An ad-hoc committee was formed among the mill operators to recommend a solution to the problem. For the interim, all team leaders were advised by memo to remove all noncalibrated personal tools from the plant until a resolution was reached. April 10.

Follow-up:

The ad-hoc committee found that it was common practice to use old calipers for rough-cutting, however, the machinists kept them in their tool box when they are not in use so the issue had never come up before. They pointed out the 99.2 percent defect-free performance in the mill area and their very low scrap rate as evidence that the practice did not detract from product quality. The committee recommended amending Standard Operating Procedure 9.037 to allow the use of noncalibrated calipers for rough-cutting. They obtained an uncontrolled copy of the procedure and marked it to include having all noncalibrated calipers permanently engraved "For Reference Only," and clearly defining under what circumstances they could be used. The draft revision was turned over to manufacturing engineering. April 28.

Follow-up:

Manufacturing Engineering released revision D to SOP 9.037. All machinists were called into a briefing on the new revision. They were reminded to request changes to SOPs when procedure did not cover how processes were actually being performed and to question all practices that were not part of documented procedures. Their feedback was that they understood more clearly the importance of regularly reviewing the SOPs and of keeping the SOPs up to date. May 12.

Follow-up:

A spot audit was conducted on June 2. Of 15 workstations audited, there were no deviations and there was evidence that the new procedure was being followed. June 4.

Follow-up:

A second spot audit was conducted on July 14. Again the audit indicated that revision D to SOP 9.037 was being followed. We reviewed the defect performance for the mill area for May and June and found that it had not changed from previous months. CAR 304 is closed and will be reviewed during the next scheduled periodic audit. July 18.

This example is interesting from several perspectives. It was good that the organization took a big-picture view to see if the problem was common throughout the organization. Taking the narrow view, the organization could have disciplined the mill operator for not using calibrated calipers. Secondly, you could ask: "Why do anything?" The uncalibrated calipers were not used to approve product and were not causing harm (in fact, the use of the calipers might have been contributing to product quality). We can only assume it's important that the operators follow procedures; the current procedures were wrong and, therefore, operators were not using them. Finally, we noticed the use of the term *spot audit* in the vernier calipers example, which we interpret as a spot check, not an audit.

Sorting the Trash: Deciding What to Do with the Bad Stuff

Another process used in the quality field is dispositioning nonconforming product. Dispositioning nonconforming product is not remedial, corrective, or preventive action. Dispositioning nonconforming product is deciding what you are going to do with the out-of-specification, broken, bad, or incorrect stuff you found (identified). Dispositioning is deciding if you are going to scrap it, dump it, reprocess it, rework it, repair it, downgrade it, or send (sell) it to the customer anyway. The requirements for dispositioning controls are covered in ISO 9001:2000, clause 8.3, Nonconforming Product Control. Do not confuse sorting the trash with any type of corrective/preventive action.

The dispositioning process would apply to service industries that provide a ready-to-use service (rental or lease of equipment) and sales service (inventory product for sale) sectors. For example, a rental car company may have nonconforming automobiles and a distributor may have damaged product that must be dispositioned.

The Internal Customer

Now you understand the corrective/preventive action process, or at least understand what you don't understand about it. You may be a customer of the corrective action process, or you may be responsible for ensuring that the process is working, either way you want to get the benefits—the pay back.

Everyone—manager, supervisor, representative, or line operator—needs to do a better job of deciding what problems are important, fixing them, and then ensuring that there are benefits. Only then will there be improvement in your organization, business, or work environment. Instead, organizations are focusing most of their energy on finding problems, no matter how trivial, and accumulating lists of them. What is worse, they claim they fixed the problem when it wasn't fixed at all. As we said in the beginning, organizations are losing big bucks because problems are not being corrected and organizational resources are being squandered on trivial issues.

In the following chapters, we will explore what needs to be done to reap the benefits for our problem (and opportunity) identification efforts and how the audit department can be improved to be part of the management team.

Summary

The following words were defined for use in this book:

Remedial Action: an action taken to alleviate the symptoms of existing nonconformities or any other undesirable situation.

Corrective Action: an action taken to eliminate the cause(s) of existing nonconformities (problems) or any other undesirable situation in order to prevent recurrence.

Preventive Action: an action taken to eliminate the cause(s) of potential nonconformities (problems) or any other undesirable situation in order to prevent occurrence.

Differentiating between corrective and preventive action can be as simple as the following:

> If you take action to eliminate the cause of a problem as a result of a reported product or service problem (nonconformity), customer complaint, or quality system audit, you are practicing corrective action (being reactive).

> If you take action to eliminate the cause of a problem as a result of *analyzing data,* you are practicing preventive action (being pro-active).

Instead of getting caught up in the quagmire of the endless discussions of corrective versus preventive, think in terms of the entire system and the processes that make up the system. Systems thinking is evaluating a process in its relationship to the related processes in the system and defining the cause(s) of the problem.

Chapter 5

Taking Action

In this chapter, we will explore several filter and evaluation steps to ensure that what you are working on is important. In many organizations, the filter step has been bypassed to get on with fixing the problem. The difficulty with bypassing this decision phase is that many corrective and preventive action programs are being overloaded with trivialities. The imperfections identified by auditors that are not system problems, neither/nor their correction will improve the process/system or provide any benefit to the organization. Rather than belittle the failures of such practices, we will discuss the Audit Function Improvement Process as an alternative to following in their footsteps.

The corrective action process is the same as the one introduced in the last chapter, but, in this chapter, we have introduced a new element. This new element is the interaction, at appropriate stages, with "those guys" who conducted the audit. We believe this to be a very important element that has been missing from the improvement actions initiated in response to audits. As you will see, this interaction between auditor and auditee is beneficial in verifying understanding in the early stages of the correction process. Waiting until all the actions have been implemented only to find out you had misunderstood the auditor's meaning is not only counterproductive, but also is an absolute waste of time and resources.

Why should it be necessary to talk to "them" when you have the audit report, the CARs, and notes from the exit meeting? During the exit meeting, the entire quality system, with all its good and bad points, is summarized by the auditors. Every time a nonconformity is mentioned, someone (or several someones) in the room grits their teeth and drops their head, thinking: "How could we have missed that?" Each time that occurs, the auditor is no longer heard, and the complete sense of what is being said is lost. The collective half-remembrances of 15 to 20 people will not be able to reconstruct what was said a half-hour after the meeting, let alone a week or more later.

So, in spite of the fact that you attended the exit meeting (and half-heard the auditors' comments), and in spite of the fact that you have a report detailing the findings or the results of the audit, it may be time for a different approach. It is true that the next step is for you and your staff to decide what you will do to address each of these findings. But this is the time for you to take a more controlled approach to the corrective action process.

Initiating Corrective Action

The Audit Function Improvement Process defines the steps necessary for you and your organization to get the most benefit from the audit function (from report to improvement). In many organizations, auditors are less than helpful during a time when they are needed most to answer the auditee's questions. The process shown in Figure 5.1 is one which will provide just the opposite impression when fully implemented and functional.

The Audit Function Improvement Process flowchart brings together all the players in the corrective/preventive action process. We will discuss each step for improvement and the connectivity between the auditor and the auditee (stakeholder of the process).

In our discussion of the Audit Function Improvement Process, we will describe this process in some detail in order to demonstrate its utility. We will apply the Audit Function Improvement Process to one of the (CARs) from your audit. We will also "break away" now and then, in sections set in shaded blocks, to review the path a corrective action team might follow.

In chapters 1 and 2, we described methods used by the audit team to prepare the audit report and the findings presented and discussed with you in the exit meeting. Whether the audit was a first-, second-, or third-party audit, all steps in this process are applicable. The first process step (see the number in the lower right corner of each box of Figure 5.1) includes only the auditors' presentation of the audit results (see Figure 5.2)

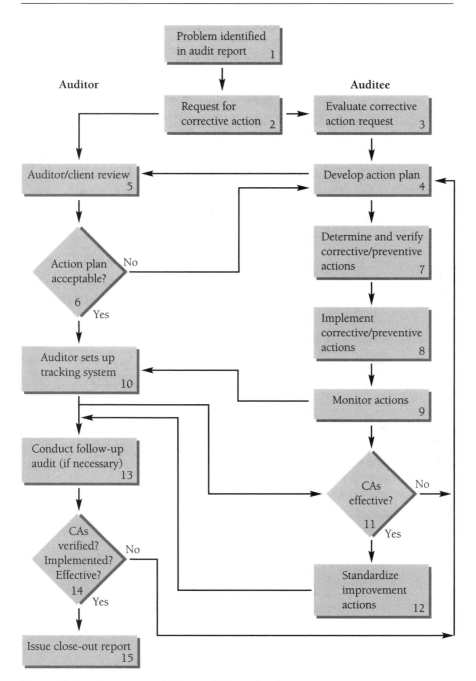

Figure 5.1. Summary of the audit function improvement process.

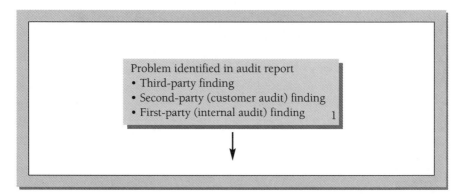

Figure 5.2. AF 1P, step 1.

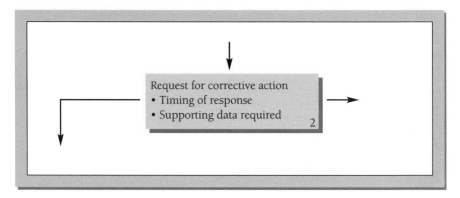

Figure 5.3. AFIP, step 2.

during the exit meeting. It is in this step that you hear the complete results of the audit. You should have been provided a daily update of the non-conformities found during the audit, but that is the equivalent of reading ten independent short segments from *War and Peace* and saying you have read the entire book. This is your opportunity to get the complete picture by asking the auditors questions about the findings and supporting evidence to ensure that you both understand and agree.

Requesting Action

In Step 2, the auditors will present you with a stack of corrective action requests CARs to review and sign. Each CAR form (see Figure 5.3) should address one finding only, not one or several nonconformities. If the auditors have handed you a CAR form (Figure 5.4) with a list of nonconformities,

CORRECTIVE ACTION REQUEST	
Date: 25 May 20XX	CAR number: 950525-03

Auditee: Our Company	
Ourtown, MI	Audit number: 950525

Finding:

    Products and materials are not adequately identified
to ensure that only materials meeting the customers'
requirements are used.

Contact	Auditor
Signature: *John B. Brannick*	Signature: *James D. Hillside*
Title: *Material Contract Mgr.*	Title: *Lead Auditor*

Remedial
Action:

Root
Cause:

Corrective
Action
Plan
(to prevent
recurrence):

Corrective Action Plan Dates:	Start	Complete	Auditor Acceptance:	Date:

Corrective
Action
Taken
(to prevent
recurrence):

Signature: _____   Date:

Corrective Action Approved [ ]	Corrective Action Disapproved [ ]	Auditor: _____

Follow-Up Audit Date: Signature: _____

Close-Out Date: Signature: _____

Figure 5.4. CAR, state the problem.

hand it back and ask them to state exactly what system failure is to be addressed. If the audit team has not stated a finding, with supporting evidence, then they have either not completed their investigation, there is not enough data to support a finding, or they want you to structure your system to suit them. In any case, refuse to sign the CAR until the auditors provide evidence.

Now we know you may be thinking that if you refuse, you have just thrown your chances of ever achieving "preferred status" out the window. Whether your organization is undergoing a first-, second-, or third-party audit, you are being audited to determine compliance with the applicable standard, not the audit team's preferences. You are responsible for achieving peak performance through the development of effective systems and processes. If your systems and processes are not effective, the evidence will be clear. But changing procedures simply to comply with an individual auditor's preference is dangerous. The danger in your compliance with the audit team's idea of "acceptable" performance that is not based on the requirements (standards, contracts) is that whenever there is a change in the audit team, there will be another insupportable finding that you have to address. Before you know it, your procedures and practices will no longer satisfy the requirements of the standard you were to comply with or worse, result in an ineffective, costly process. If, on the other hand, the audit team presents you with CARs requesting action on findings for which there is supporting evidence and that reflect valid system concerns, then the need for corrective action will be understood and accepted without argument. Disappointment, maybe, but no arguments.

The CAR in Figure 5.4 is just such an example. In this instance (Case 1, chapter 2, page 31), disappointment wins over argument. The "how" and "where" have been demonstrated by pointing out that the auditor's guides witnessed each observed nonconformity during the audit. "Auditor's luck" might have been argued on one, or possibly two, of the occurrences, but not ten! There is just too much evidence that there is a system failure to be corrected.

Your discussion with the auditors about the timing of the CAR response should not be misconstrued as the completion date for the corrective action. This is the time required to investigate the finding and identify the corrective actions to be taken. The auditors do not expect an immediate answer, but you should not expect the response time to be unlimited either. Unless you have a large number of findings, the auditors will expect this initial response in two to four weeks. When you do send your response, you should also provide supporting information (control charts, cause-and-effect diagrams, Pareto charts, trend charts, flowcharts, etc.) with each CAR. This information will be the basis for you to demonstrate that your corrective actions are effective.

Audit Program Manager

In order to ensure effective results, audit findings should be filtered by the person managing the audit process. All programs utilizing resources and issuing reports that will consume resources should be managed and be accountable for their performance. The audit manager should evaluate the findings to ensure that they are clear, correct, complete, and effectively written. Assuming they pass the first test (see chapters 1 and 2 for details), the findings should also be checked to ensure that they are consistent with the organization's goals. The person who authorized the audit (the client) should review the report and make decisions either to request improvement actions or not to request action based on the organizational objectives, the risk involved, the available data, and personal knowledge and experience.

Whatever the decision, a record should be kept for the audit file. There is a general problem-solving rule that is applicable here:

> Whenever there is a decision made or an action taken in regard to a corrective action, the basis for that decision or action must be recorded, as well as the method for monitoring effectiveness.

By documenting these decisions, actions, and monitoring methods, you have established that formal corrective and preventive action investigations have been initiated on valid concerns. At the same time, you will also need to document the business reasons for prioritizing the corrective actions as you have. It is natural for managers to think in terms of customer demands, project deadlines, costs of implementation, and available resources with hardly a pause to consider writing anything down, but you will find that the lack of this one piece of evidence will result in countless headaches later when you try to demonstrate that you had good reasons for postponing or delaying action.

The audit manager could act as traffic cop. He could stop the report and hand it back to the author to better define the extent of the problem. In our earlier example citing the forms control problem, it would be appropriate to hand the report back to the auditor to get any additional facts to determine the extent of the problem. The auditor should be responsible for taking into account the perceived significance of the findings from audits and evaluations. The report should not just be a laundry list and it is up to you, the audit manager, to ensure you get as much relevant information as possible. There is no standard method or guideline for evaluating the importance of findings other than those stated previously. But then there is no reason why you cannot or should not contact the auditor and request additional information to aid you in this process.

There could be several valid business reasons for not initiating new corrective actions in response to an audit finding (such as the forms control problem). The audit manager could be privy to information that new software was just purchased to control all forms via the computer network. In this case, the audit manager could enter this information in the plan for action and be done with it, but, of course, this would not be the correct thing to do. The audit manager should pass on the finding to the project team installing the new forms software to ensure the new forms generation program complies with QM 5.05. It is also possible for the auditors to uncover problems that you are not interested in solving because your previous attempts have proven corrective actions uneconomical and of no benefit to the organization, and you will, of course, have the records to prove it. In either case, there will be data available to demonstrate that the corrective actions have been investigated prior to the audit.

In some organizations, the culture requires that the audit manager review all findings and/or opportunities prior to forwarding them to the process owner (stakeholder). In the government, "staff" groups cannot tell "line" groups what to do. Therefore, the staff group, who usually does the audits (assessments), must pass on their report to a series of administrative levels before it finally lands on the process owner's desk, often several months later.

There are a myriad of problems/opportunities with a myriad of scenarios, so there must be human judgment (intervention) along the way. In fact, only one out of ten problems/opportunities may be a "big deal" (addressing the issue will result in a big pay back to the organization). But when you find one, it is well worth the effort to solve the problem or take advantage of the opportunity to ensure your organization continues to prosper. Remember the old saying: "If it was easy, everybody would be doing it!"

Direct Requests for Action

The most common practice is for the lead auditor to simply hand over completed CAR or nonconformance forms to the auditee at the end of the audit. The report automatically goes from the auditor to the process owner (auditee) for consideration with the agreement that there will be a response at some future date. Sending reported findings directly to the process owners is fine, if the process owners have an equal say and have been trained in techniques to evaluate the requests to correct problems or requests to launch programs to secure opportunities. There is value in initiation of action in this manner, not only to reduce improvement process cycle time, but also to ensure the issue is addressed to prevent future customer concerns. The process owner should then evaluate the request for action just as we discussed in the previous section.

SIDEBAR

> Many organizations are finding it necessary for management to review audit reports prior to sending them to the manager of the area audited. Management (quality manager, audit program manager, client) reviews the finding to ensure it is clearly stated, is correct and is value added. This is not just a formality, but an important decision step.

Code Blue

The corrective/preventive action program timing should remain flexible at all times. There are two reasons for this:

1. Some actions take longer than others (a capital request may be required).
2. Some actions are so important that resources should be assigned to the problem/opportunity immediately.

The corrective/preventive action review process should never be so rigid and bureaucratic that the process steps become more important than taking action. Certainly, one major potential downfall of an ISO 9001 quality system is that people tend to become focused on the internal process and forget the organization's performance objectives. There needs to be some type of fast-track process for really important stuff. If a major customer has a major problem you don't say: "Thank you for bringing this issue to our attention. We will write this up to initiate our corrective action process. Based on our current backlog, we should be getting back to you in two weeks." Similarly, if findings point out stuff that is costing the organization big bucks or big-time opportunities are identified, you can't afford to treat these the same as you would one illegible calibration sticker problem.

For example, when a customer reports the receipt of nonconforming parts, the concern should not go to the bottom of the manufacturing concerns to be addressed. After verifying the part number, quantity, lot number, etc., the following might occur:

- Key personnel are immediately provided the available information.
- Delivery of parts is halted.
- Management visits customer to outline corrective action.
- Simultaneous inspection of finished and production parts is initiated.
- Inspection data are recorded and analyzed.
- Remedial, or containment, actions are determined (such as sorting the good stuff from the bad stuff).
- Remedial actions are recorded and implemented.
- A team is selected to address this issue.
- All information, data, and recorded actions are passed to the team.
- Team initiates investigation to define the problem and complete the corrective action process.

All these things may occur in a relatively short time. That is not to say that these actions should be rushed. We have observed some instances where these steps were completed in about two hours, but in others, several weeks were required to complete these same steps.

Just as there are issues that must be addressed immediately, there are issues that will take a long time to fix (that is, new technology or capital will be needed). Long-term issues should not be forced into an artificial, preset schedule. Instead, your corrective action process should require regular updates on the progress of both long-term issues and short-term corrective actions. More often than not, it is not the corrective action practices that are at fault, but the documentation and follow-up of the actions taken. The longer the process takes, the greater the probability of losing focus on the actions to be completed.

Evaluate Requests: Stakeholder

The third step in the process, evaluating corrective action requests (Figure 5.5), is the one you (the stakeholder) are about to begin now that the auditors have left. This element is a very important step toward the suc-

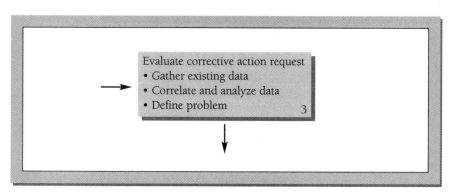

Figure 5.5. AFIP, step 3.

cess of this process. As did the previous step, this one also includes data gathering, analyzing data, and possibly restating the problem or opportunity. You should understand that even though you have accepted the responsibility for the CARs, you are not obligated to initiate action for each one. That is, you have a choice in determining which items will be addressed first, and, depending on the data you gather to support your claim, you may find that no action at all is required. This is fundamentally true no matter what quality system standard is to be applied. Understanding that this particular stance may seem to be just a bit radical for auditors to be taking in regard to corrective action, we would like to remind you of the wording of ISO 9001:2000, clause 8.5.2:

> The Organization shall take corrective to eliminate the cause of nonconformities in order to prevent recurrence. Corrective shall be appropriate to the impact of the problems encountered.[9]
>
> *Note: Risk, or impact in the above, is the probability that an event or action may adversely affect the organization or activity under audit.*[10]

In other words, corrective action is your decision, but it is also your responsibility to document the reason for your decision. You might also note that it is not uncommon for the evidence gathered in an audit by the auditors to misrepresent (unintentionally) the actual practice. Before you get excited, let us list just a few of the reasons why such an "unlikely" event might occur:

1. The auditee doesn't listen to the entire question before framing a response, thus providing an answer contrary to the actual practice.

2. Auditees provide incomplete answers, believing that auditors' questions must be answered, but information must never be volunteered.

3. Words are defined differently by the auditee and auditor.

4. The auditor frames the question incorrectly for the auditee's understanding.

5. The auditee is intimidated by the auditor.

6. The auditee fears being fired for anything found wrong during the audit.

7. The auditee responds without knowing the facts.

8. The auditor does not verify all the information received during the audit.

With the possible exception of Item 2, none of these is done to intentionally mislead the auditor, provide incorrect information, or to trick the auditee. In addition, you might be reminded that auditors base their decision that a nonconformance exists on a sampling of all available evidence, and then base their findings on that data. You should also bear in mind that most of their findings are correct, even if they do involve your own pet project. That small percentage of the time when the auditors are misled by the evidence provided should neither cause you to conclude that the process is not worthwhile, nor should it cause you to initiate action where none is needed. You have the right to "stop work" if continued work on a problem will not result in a benefit to the organization. The first thing you should do is collect additional information to determine the magnitude of the problem.

We can demonstrate what we mean by examining one of six findings identified by a third-party registrar in a recent audit:

> *Finding: Although the operating procedures for manufacturing are considered satisfactory, they have not been formatted in the formal style required by QM 5.05. The same also applies to the forms used by the distribution department.*

From this statement you cannot tell how important the correction of this nonconformance is to your organization. In fact, there are several questions that may be asked, including:

- Are the revision levels in the left-hand corner instead of the right-hand corner as required by QM 5.05?

- Is the information incomplete and resulting in confusion when information is passed on to other departments?

- Are the records wrong or incomplete?
- Does if affect external or internal customers?
- Are these two departments the only two examples identified out of all the departments using the 257 forms in the quality system?
- Is QM 5.05 relevant in these examples or is another procedure applicable?

While it may be true that you have to correct this issue to re-register your organization, you must first determine if it is just an isolated problem, or a problem throughout the organization that is affecting performance? You don't know at this point in time! You have to investigate and evaluate the results before you commit your organization's resources to corrective actions.

In order for you to make the proper decisions, you need to gather data and information from sources throughout your organization, including:

- The auditors who conducted the audit
- The associates interviewed by the auditors
- Process control data
- Quality control data
- Customer corrective actions
- Inventory control data
- Training records
- Internal nonconformance reports
- Internal audit reports
- Customer audit reports
- Field performance data
- Inspection and test data
- Corrective actions that were begun before the audit

Reviewing information from sources such as these before jumping feet first into corrective action will save time and resources for the following reasons:

1. You will not need to allocate new resources nor lose time by beginning a new investigation if you have a team working on corrective actions that will resolve the finding with no or only slight modification to their corrective action plan.

2. As we demonstrated earlier, auditors do not always receive all the information needed to verify compliance, so a quick recheck

with the appropriate function can prevent an unnecessary and costly allocation of resources.

3. The information you gather from these sources can be given directly to corrective action team, saving valuable time by providing information to help better define the problem to be solved.

4. You will avoid allocating resources incorrectly to address a finding that has been misunderstood.

As we said before, you must use all the information at your disposal to ensure that the findings are not only valid, but also that they are understood to take effective corrective action. This was demonstrated in a recent audit when the auditee was addressing a finding related to processing nonconforming product. Although both the finding and supporting non-conformance statements were thought to be understood by the auditee when the audit results were presented during the exit interview, a quick verification with the auditor a few days afterward revealed that the intended procedure change was insufficient to correct and maintain the system. The *auditor provided the necessary clarification* to the plant contact by telephone before the corrective actions had been initiated, preventing both ineffective corrective action and an additional nonconformance which would have occurred in a future audit.

SIDEBAR

In one *After the Audit* class an auditor shared with us that he used his network and contacts to help auditees with corrective action from time to time. In one case, he just finished an audit of Carol's area and knew she had been waiting several months for a certain piece of equipment to complete a corrective action. The auditor called Jane, the head of the department that supplied the equipment, and told her of Carol's plight. The corrective action was closed the next day.

Now, you may think that doing all this will take a considerable amount of time. Of course, it will take some time, but this investigation is intended to be conducted only to the degree necessary to ensure that you have the data required to develop action plans and allocate resources. It is not intended to provide all the information required to correct the finding. Although it is only the preliminary review phase, these steps are essential for you to make the proper corrective action team assignments and will save false starts and repeated steps later.

As the corrective action teams begin their assignments, they will be better informed because you have taken the time to provide them with relevant information about the finding along with the CAR. Not only will this provide motivation for the team because they understand that these corrective actions are worthwhile, it will save them a tremendous amount of time gathering information to properly define the problem.

We can hear you now saying: "What? The finding is the problem as defined by the auditors. That is the problem the team must solve." To that, we can only reply that you are right—and wrong. You are right because the corrective actions initiated as a result of the CAR must prove that the finding has been effectively corrected. However, you are wrong because the finding statement may very well understate the magnitude of the true problem.

Auditors, you see, are a conservative lot. As such, they tend to state findings in the simplest, the most tactful, and the most defensible form for the evidence in hand. They know quite well the advantages—and dangers—of sampling techniques, and their findings, you will remember, are based on information "samples" from your quality system. So, then, your corrective action teams must gather, correlate, and analyze even more data to properly define the problem that is to be solved.

The team will define the problem to be solved on your own internal corrective action form. As long as their data show that the finding will be resolved by determining the best solution for the problem they have defined, you have nothing to fear. Besides, the CAR form (see Figure 5.4) does not ask how you define the problem, but requires you to state what is being done (remedial action), the root cause, etc. The only thing the team needs to remember is to keep records of their data, analysis, and actions taken at each step of the process. The team's problem statement, because it is based on a larger database, will provide the team with the focus necessary to define their next steps.

Developing Action Plans: Stakeholder

A good problem statement should be clear and concise, yet state the problem in quantifiable terms. Inherent in the problem statement, as defined by the team, will be "sub-problems" that must be resolved by the team. Before the team begins to initiate corrective action, an action plan will need to be developed. For the team's corrective actions to be most effective, these "subplots" will have to be arranged so that each is addressed in proper order. Some actions, like remedial actions, for example, will have to be initiated immediately to prevent continued effects of the problem from impacting the processes, the system, and the customer.

Some organizations require the auditor to complete these action plans and then have them reviewed by the sponsor (the manager whose function is most affected by the finding). These are the organizations that have the least effective audit programs and the lowest opinion of the value of internal and external assessments. We have already pointed out the danger to an organization's taking such shortcuts. The corrective actions taken will not be very effective because the actions taken will be based on incomplete data. Not only will the corrective actions be less effective, another problem will arise in the next audit because the auditor, contrary to the ISO 10011-1, clause 7 statement that it is the auditee who has ownership of problems,[11] will be taking responsibility for this function's corrective actions rather than maintaining the required independence (see ISO 10011-1, clause 4.3).[12] These organizations have so little faith in the audit function that they want to minimize any involvement of the people operating the processes so they can remain focused on the "important stuff." Fortunately for you, their competitors, these organizations will not benefit from their audit program, and will continue to be plagued by ineffective corrective actions. For your corrective action team and the stakeholders in this process, however, the result will be different because the action plan will address each of the dependent issues which must be resolved to provide a complete and effective solution.

In our case (see Figure 5.4), the problem definition is not a simple matter. There are many different areas to consider as indicated by the supporting evidence:

1. Product samples in the storage area are not identified in any manner.

2. Process sheets indicate material that failed the stated test requirements is passed without authorization or comment.

3. The Final Test Plan/Procedure does not specify that finished product shall have passed earlier inspections and test.

4. Nonconforming material in storage areas is not clearly identified as to status.

5. The disposition of nonconforming material is specified in Nonconforming Control Procedure 213.012, 4.6, as the Technical Manager, in contradiction with paragraph 4.2 of the same document.

6. The disposition of material in NCP 213.012, 4.8, lists three options for disposition, yet the Material Review Board Report lists five options.

7. Product in the nonconforming material storage is not identified.

8. The table for classification of materials for RPT Process is blank (IC 206.003, 4.7).

9. The methods for periodic verification of materials in procedure IC 206.003, 4.8, are undefined.

10. There are no procedures for control of customer-supplied product, yet it is reported that one customer provides materials for processing and return.

The supporting evidence is the starting point in defining the problem. Here we will find the clues that should direct the team's focus. In the above list of nonconformities, for example, the material concerns fall into the two general groupings of material identification and procedural issues:

Unidentified: Raw material storage (#1)

Nonconforming material storage (#4, 7)

Procedures: Test procedure incomplete (#3)

Test procedure not followed (#2)

Materials classification table blank (#8)

Contradictory information (#5, 6)

Undefined verification process (#9)

Not prepared (#10)

Although this is a simple grouping, it does indicate that there are conflicting, or at least inconsistent, material handling practices. The team now has three areas to begin gathering data: inventory storage, material handling practices, and material handling/test procedures. Team members split up to gather information from these areas to help define the problem. They returned with flowcharts of the material handling throughout the system and material storage. They also have records of a number of observed practices which do not meet customer requirements. Evaluating the results of their efforts, they defined the problem as:

Material handling and control practices result in 19 percent of reported scrap and 28 percent of customer complaints.

You will notice that the team's definition differs from the finding stated in the audit report. The team members have analyzed their data to state the magnitude of the problem in its definition. The values also represent the initial measure of current performance and are connected to organizational objectives (scrap levels and customer satisfaction). Wow! Maybe we need to do something about this.

The team members were not side-tracked by stating the causes, but only stated these inconsistent practices as a fact. The determination of root cause will come later. Why there are inconsistent practices is to be determined during the root-cause analysis. While some of the team members may think the answer is obvious, others are not convinced that a simple answer exists. They have agreed to gather the data necessary to determine the cause and base their decisions on those facts. As yet, there is not enough data to identify the root cause, but they have made a good start.

Before the team's corrective action plan can be developed, there are several other steps to be completed (see Figure 5.6). The corrective action team needs to gather additional data to determine the root cause or causes for the defined problem. The root cause is the original event which triggered the initial problem resulting in the system deficiency. The team will apply basic problem-solving tools such as Pareto charts, cause-and-effect diagrams, etc., to determine the root cause. When the team has identified

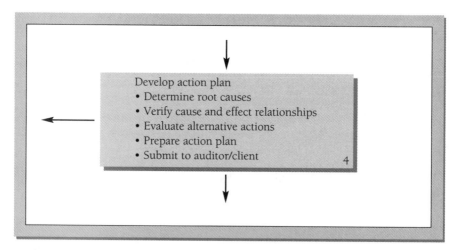

Figure 5.6. AFIP, step 4.

the root cause (or causes), the team members will test the cause-and-effect relationships identified to verify their results. Using process data gathered by the members, the team will begin evaluating alternative actions that their evidence indicates will provide the desired solution to the defined problem. They may have to conduct additional tests, gather additional data, and analyze the results to make the proper selection, but the team's effectiveness depends on the effective application of their data analysis skills. When the team is satisfied with the results, the action plan may be prepared.

The team member's investigations have provided evidence that there are several different procedures governing material handling. Some are very lax, while one is very specific. While the existence of differing procedures is supporting evidence of the defined problem, it is not the cause. They will have to dig further to find out why so that the problem can be resolved. For example, the team members need a little more information:

- Which of the methods contained in the various procedures is correct?
- Are the procedures, as written, incorrect, or are the practices?
- Could both the procedures and the practices be incorrect?
- Where in the process is scrap occurring?

In order to answer these questions, the team will need to prepare a flowchart of each of the procedures as written. As they prepare the flowcharts of these procedures, they are careful to note the information received, the process to be performed, and the final output of each process. They will also need to analyze process data to determine where the scrap is found and reported.

The team members begin to identify "gaps" in the written procedures. They also find that there are "gaps" in the actual practices which do not match the gaps in the documented procedures. As they conduct further comparisons, they find that contradictory instructions do not account for all the inconsistent practices. The breaks in the flowcharts appear at interfaces in the system where materials must pass from one department or process to another, or from stores for processing and return. In order to determine whether or not their observations are consistent with the auditors' findings in the audit, the team contacts the lead auditor to find out each point at which each nonconformity was noted during the audit. The auditor's response confirms the team's conclusions regarding the six key nonconformities (see nonconformity numbers 1, 2, 4, 7, 9, and 10 listed earlier). When they cross-reference this information with the location of reported scrap problems, they find that their conclusions are consistent with the audit and process data.

Closer examination reveals that there were five different areas of the plant involved in the development of these procedures. That, in itself, does not provide the reason for the occurrence of the observed problems. When the history of the different procedures is unraveled, the team begins to understand the magnitude and complexity of their problem. They find that the procedures were developed by each department as the plant expanded. The three processing departments developed their own procedures, while the raw material storage and finished goods storage developed their own. In addition, the engineering group had no procedures for long-term storage of test materials, whether or not the materials are later introduced into production. While this might have been an acceptable practice when the plant was small, as the plant grew, these engineering samples became mixed with, and often confused with, other raw materials as there was no separate storage area for such samples.

The team prepares an action plan to be submitted to the auditor with the updated CAR (Figure 5.7). They choose to prepare a simple action plan format as it contains all the necessary information. They plan to have the procedures revised in four to five weeks. They also plan to allow time to gather data to verify that their actions are effective. They will provide the auditor with an additional update at regular intervals.

The action plan itself may be formal, as a Gantt chart or PERT chart, or it may be a simple table stating the actions to be taken, the individual responsible for each, and the completion date. The actual form varies by organization, but the form is not as important as the results. The team will fill in the space provided on the CAR form with their remedial actions taken, the root cause identified, and a brief statement of their planned corrective actions. The date the action is initiated and the planned completion date should also be provided to the auditor by the stakeholder.

Acknowledge Action Plans: Auditor

When the investigations for all the CAR forms are complete to this stage, they should be sent to the auditor or other designated person for review and approval (Figure 5.8). Typically, only the form itself is sent to the

CORRECTIVE ACTION REQUEST	
Date: 25 May 20XX	CAR number: 950525-03

Auditee: Our Company	
Ourtown, MI	Audit number: 950525

Finding:

Products and materials are not adequately identified to ensure that only materials meeting the customers' requirements are used.

Contact	Auditor
Signature: *John B. Brannick*	Signature: *James D. Hillside*
Title: *Material Contract Mgr.*	Title: *Lead Auditor*

Remedial
Action: 1. Segregate all unidentified products and raw materials.
2. Set up reevaluation process for all such materials prior to use.

Root Conflicting procedures: purchasing, control of non-
Cause: conforming product, raw material control, and process test procedures.

Corrective 1. Reevaluate processes involved to ensure that
Action   requirements are understood.
Plan 2. Revise each of the procedures involved.
(to prevent 3. Include purchasing, engineering, manufacturing, and
recurrence):   quality departments on future document reviews.

Corrective   Start   Complete
Action   Auditor
Plan Dates: June 5, 20XX July 30, 20XX Acceptance: Date:

Corrective
Action
Taken
(to prevent
recurrence):

Signature: _____   Date:

Corrective   Corrective
Action   Action
Approved [   ] Disapproved [   ]   Auditor: _____

Follow-Up Audit Date: _____   Signature: _____

Close-Out Date: _____   Signature: _____

Figure 5.7. CAR, action plan.

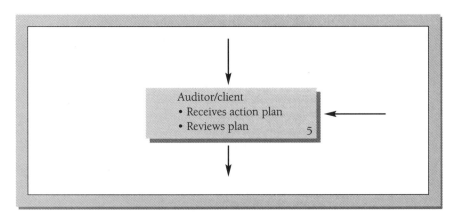

Figure 5.8. AFIP, step 5.

auditor or designated person. However, you may find that providing a summary of the supporting data will be more convincing for the reviewer. This step only requires that the auditor or other designated person, check out the action plans developed by the stakeholders (owners of the problem). The review of the action plan is required for third-party audits, and may or may not be required for internal audits. A designated individual may be the auditor, lead auditor, assigned reviewer, audit program manager, client, improvement manager, quality manager, and so on. In this section and the remainder of the chapter, we refer to auditor duties, but those duties may be assigned to other designated individuals depending on the organization culture.

Of course, the audit manager should have more than a casual interest in the actions to be taken. The audit manager, being responsible for providing resources, will need to know how his resources are being utilized. If the action plan presents a conflict with other plans, there may need to be adjustments. The audit manager might also be aware of other actions, planned or in progress, which may support your actions while preventing a duplication of effort. The audit manager will also require regular updates to monitor the progress of the process owner's implementation of the action plan. This ongoing exchange of information is to ensure that the implementation program is working and effective.

The audit program functions more effectively when it is a common practice for the process owner to submit plans (corrective action plans) for review as an element of control of the improvement process. The auditor who issued the corrective action request (or designed individual) should determine if the root cause you have identified and the stated corrective action plan are consistent with the stated finding. This may seem to be simply a matter of acknowledgment of the action to be taken. However, this review serves several purposes:

1. It ensures the consistency of the corrective actions taken with the finding.
2. It provides baseline data which will serve later as a baseline to verify improvement.
3. It provides the timing for the completion of the corrective action plan.

The reviewer may know enough about your system to be able to accept your stated root cause and the corrective action plan as stated without additional information. Face-value acceptance is dependent more upon the nature of the finding than the reviewer's knowledge of your system. It is for this reason that we strongly recommend that supporting evidence be provided. Not only will this information aid with the understanding of the root cause determination, it will also provide the links of the root cause to the corrective action plan and to the resolution of the finding. If you have invested the time and resources to gather the information necessary to identify the root cause, analyzed and selected the possible corrective actions, and then developed a plan for their implementation, why not use it to good advantage? Besides, if the auditor (reviewer) does understand your system and also has analytical skills that you lack, then this same auditor who identified the system weakness may also point out a weakness in your evaluation process. In that case, the auditor becomes an asset to your organization as an additional resource in this Audit Function Improvement Process.

We must advise caution in this type of auditor-auditee interchange. It is very true that this partnership with the auditor is an excellent utilization of the available knowledge and experience. However, the auditor must exercise caution so that any comments made are not misconstrued as an order or directive that may be interpreted by the auditee as: "We have to do it this way because the auditor said so!" In order to maintain the required independence in this step, the auditor must only evaluate the information provided. In doing so, the auditor's comments should be limited to "accept" or "reject," although it is reasonable that the basis for a "reject" could be provided. If your organization is small, the auditor may be expected to act as an internal consultant to the owner of the process, but the auditor must not assume responsibility for the corrective action even then. One organization assigns auditors to various departments of

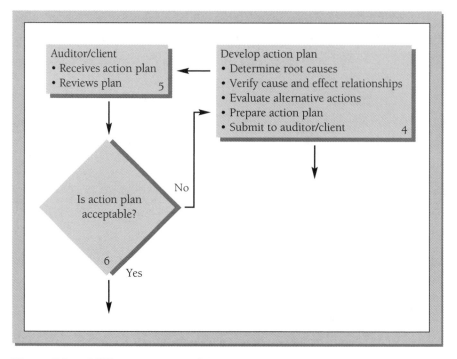

Figure 5.9. AFIP, steps 4, 5, and 6.

the organization to act as a consultant for that area. Of course, they are not allowed to audit the area for which they are consulting, due to the conflicts of interest.

There are times when findings involve only the preparation or completion of procedures. These are remedial actions which require only the revision or development of those documents. In that case, you will be providing a plan for the completion of those documents, and the statement of root cause may not be necessary. The corrective action plan (Figure 5.9) may be a simple statement that the relevant documents will be completed with the timing for their completion. The auditor will normally accept these as written, but will verify the implementation of these revisions or new procedures at the next audit. In the meantime, your plan should include provisions to monitor the implementation and effectiveness of these procedures.

The primary responsibility of the auditor (reviewer) is to ensure that the root cause and corrective actions are consistent with the finding. The reviewer's (auditor's) role is not to approve the corrective actions identified by your teams. Approval of corrective action is the responsibility of the stakeholders. The auditor's role is to review the root cause and the corrective action plan contained in the CAR along with the supporting evidence provided to verify the appropriate links to the finding. The auditor will verify that the actions address issues relevant to the finding and are adequate to provide a complete solution. The supporting information you provide will demonstrate not only the thoroughness of your investigations, but also that the actions taken will be both complete and adequate. In other words, you have addressed the finding with a solution that will correct the deficiency while preventing the recurrence of the problem. There may be times, however, that the auditor (reviewer) does not agree that you have addressed the correct system concern. For example, in response to a finding addressing the disagreement between documented procedures and actual practice, the auditor may not accept the adequacy of your reissuing an update of the procedure as corrective action. What the auditor expects in this situation is evidence that the:

- Current practice has been thoroughly reviewed for adequacy
- Correct practice has been determined: as documented, as practiced, or a modification of both
- Cause of the current system variation has been identified
- Correction plan to prevent recurrence of the system variation is adequate

If this information has not been provided to the auditor, the corrective action plan will not be accepted. When the corrective action plan is not acceptable, the auditor will contact you to discuss its deficiencies. The discussion should include an explanation of the plan's unacceptability and what must be done to resolve these concerns. Your response will be to re-evaluate the corrective action plan. When you have addressed the auditor's concerns, you may resubmit the revised plan for re-evaluation.

When the auditor (reviewer) agrees that the actions are acceptable to correct the problem and prevent recurrence, the signed corrective action will be acknowledged (Figure 5.7, auditor acceptance). At the same time, the auditor (or designated person) will develop a table for tracking progress as updates are received (Figure 5.10). These updates will aid both the auditor and the auditee. The auditee will be providing evidence of the improvement actions and the auditor (audit program manager) will determine the need for a follow-up audit. Also, the auditor may act as an additional resource to review and evaluate the continued effectiveness of your corrective actions as these updates are received.

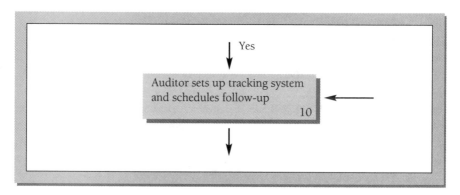

Figure 5.10. AFIP, step 10.

All this activity has not resulted in the implementation of any corrective action. The team members have been focused on the evaluation of the process. They have been gathering information which would help them decide what must be done to effectively address the finding. So now the team is ready to implement the action plan. But there is one other thing they need to do: re-evaluate their resources. Before moving on to the next step, the team sponsor should determine:

- Do the team members have the skills to carry out the assignment?
- Have the proper resources been identified?
- Are there any related systems not represented on the team that will be affected by the team's actions?
- Does the team sponsor control the outcome?

If the answer to all the above is "Yes," then the team should proceed. If not, then the team's membership should be re-evaluated and adjusted as necessary. Although radical changes to team membership are rare, resource personnel are often identified to assist the team. Just as providing the correct tools enhances the quality of the output, team members having the correct mix of skills achieve a higher level of performance. One simple test is to ask: "Does each team member have direct input into or control of the process involved?" If the answer is "No," then the team members may not be able to provide the desired skills.

This evaluation of the team's membership is necessary for effective corrective action. When the team begins the corrective action process, the problem has not yet been clearly defined. As the team progresses beyond the analysis of root cause, the skills required to solve the problem may well have changed. If that is the case, the team's membership should be re-evaluated by the team leader, the sponsor, and the team facilitator. Changing team members should be done with caution. The team members have functioned well up to this point, and change may be necessary, but could also be detrimental to the team as a whole. It may be possible that the team could effectively resolve the concern with additional resources in the form of skilled personnel to act as advisors or subject matter experts to the team. If so, providing such resources as necessary may be all that is required.

The initial analysis of root cause has been done, but now the records of that analysis should be reviewed by the team to help determine the corrective actions to be implemented. There is only one catch—it is not always that simple. The fact that a root cause has been identified does not mean that the corrective and preventive actions are obvious to all, or any, of the team members. For that reason, the team needs to gather additional information in order to confirm the root cause, which also means we are beginning to sound like a broken record. If you will remember the example of the lamp in chapter 3, you will understand why it is important to re-examine the system.

You might begin this system review by determining the input and output of each process to identify the possibilities. A good way to do this is to flowchart the process. When you flowchart the process before making changes, you may find that it is not working as it should be. Be careful to flowchart the process as it is, not as you know it ought to be. The actual practice may not follow the documented procedures, and identifying each deviation from the expected practice provides another clue to the root cause.

Time out! Wasn't root cause analysis completed already? Yes, it was. So the flowcharts, cause-and-effect diagrams, and other data should be available for your team to review as alternative actions are evaluated. The primary reason for gathering data and keeping records is so that the team will have a complete history of actions and events. As the team discusses alternative actions, the question that must be asked is: "Are we sure that the identified root cause is correct?" You may have to test several alternatives, but how do you select the most appropriate alternatives without data verifying the root cause is correct? This is not a time to be guessing. Use data, not opinion, as the basis for your team decisions.

The team leader asked the sponsor to allow another member to join the team as a representative from purchasing was included on the team. The team members realize that when they have attempted corrective actions in the past, they have only been addressing the symptoms rather than the cause. The current case is different, so far. However, they may again fall into the same trap if they do not evaluate the validity of their previous decisions as they bring their new team member up to date.

The team agrees that the root cause identified is correct and that the outlined course of action is correct. Their actions will include the standardization of methods through all the affected processes. The team members from the various departments begin rewriting procedures to overcome the deficiencies and gaps that were identified in the team's analysis. The flowcharts help them trace through the process to test the actions and verify the results. As these flowcharts are reviewed by the team, the team members begin to identify alternative actions to prevent potential problems from occurring. They look for the types of problems originally identified and extend beyond those to possible system failures as the organization continues to grow. Each of these is tested as they are developed, but the team can only test each on a very limited basis under controlled conditions.

The testing done after the actions have been selected are much like lab tests. Tests may include a try-out of one element of the process, one line, prototype test, or simulations of the process, etc. These are very short duration tests of a limited nature to verify the team's theory. Will the action stop the occurrence of the problem during the short test? By alternately starting and stopping the action, does the effect return? If so, then you have identified the correct root cause and the corrective action should be effective—as far as it goes. There are still potential problems that may occur and preventive actions to identify prior to implementation.

The team has identified as many of these potential concerns as they can, but they can only verify them under controlled conditions. What will happen under normal conditions may be another matter. By allowing for the types of problems that occur under normal production pressures, the team's limited tests may seem complete, but without a "test of fire," the results cannot be fully verified.

This next step is comparable to the "Do" step of PDCA. All the work performed so far has been in preparation of this step. Now is the time for the team to take the actions identified out into the real world for a complete test of all the elements. Before they begin, the team leader should check with the management to ensure that there have been no unforeseen changes to the action plan. There should be no problems, but there are conflicts that arise occasionally from customers' requests or schedule changes that could delay your team a few days or so. Keep in mind that this step is the implementation of your corrective and preventive actions as a test, not permanent application. This "field test" is necessary for the team to gather data to prove the effectiveness of the corrective and preventive actions. The process measures to be recorded must be identified before the test begins. In other words, the team's expectations must be recorded for comparison to the actual results.

Preparation for this test includes a re-evaluation of the actions to prevent recurrence. Have all possible actions to prevent recurrence been considered? Is there a related process or system that will be negatively affected by planned changes to the process or system? If adjustments are necessary, now is the best time to make them. Otherwise, the test may have to be repeated.

The team prepares to test the corrective and preventive actions, but in order to test on a small scale, the team selects a single process of moderate complexity that has demonstrated the problems they are trying to resolve. The team has identified the measures necessary to validate their actions, and has monitored the process to establish the current performance levels of each desired process characteristic. Prior to implementing the corrective and preventive actions, the team gets permission to train the personnel affected in the new methods. Each process check point is given the name of a team member to contact if there are any problems encountered during the test period.

Of particular interest to the team are the points of intersection between two departments. These are the interfaces where the team found problems had most often occurred. The team has emphasized the correction of those previous problems as well as the prevention of problems at these points. In order to determine the effectiveness of these actions, the team has designated check points between departments and operations for evaluating results. With one last check to ensure that everything is ready, the team implements the corrective/preventive actions.

Monitoring the results of the corrective/preventive actions is a relatively simple matter. You should remember, however, that not only must the information to be gathered be agreed upon beforehand, but also the method of analysis. The performance levels to be achieved for the actions to be acceptable should also be stated before the corrective and preventive actions are implemented. The measurement and analysis in many cases is a straightforward matter, but that is not always the case. Sometimes sophisticated statistical techniques are required. As the method of handling data might be a concern for some team members, decide beforehand how the data should be analyzed and what statistical tests, if any, might be applied. The team will gather process data from various points in the process for analysis. After the results have been reviewed, they may be summarized for reporting to the auditor (designated management representative). The frequency of these updates will depend on the timing for the follow-up audit. If the follow-up audit is three months after the team has implemented the corrective action, for example, updates might be provided at two week intervals. The auditor (designated management representative) could ask for clarification if the data provided is unclear.

Of course, it is possible that not quite everything will go according to plan. There may be any number of possibilities that could occur to cause the auditor to question the information provided. If there is a concern, the auditor might ask the team to provide additional data. After all, the purpose of this review is to help the team ensure that the corrective actions address the findings. The auditor's concern may be a simple question regarding the way the data is presented or was evaluated. If these concerns are minor, the auditor and the team may agree that no modifications to the actions are required. However, there may be times when the auditor is able to identify additional actions that should be implemented as well as those identified by the team. In that case, the team would go back to the point where they developed their original action plan to re-evaluate their data and actions through to this stage. With the records of the process evaluations the team has maintained through this process, it is very likely that they have already considered the auditor's point. An explanation may easily be provided to the auditor by relaying the necessary information and process data.

Having satisfied the auditor, the team has only to complete their "test" to prove their actions effective. The interactions experienced through this trial will either verify their decisions and actions, or they will identify weaknesses or possibly omissions. Either way, the team and the organization win. There will be more to do when these actions are to be standardized for the entire organization, but that is a discussion we will take up in the next chapter.

Summary

For the audit function to benefit an organization, there must be a mechanism for the review and evaluation of the corrective action requests resulting from audits. The Audit Function Improvement Process contains several filter and evaluation steps to ensure that what you are working on is important. Too often, the filter step is bypassed to get on with fixing the problem. As a result, the corrective and preventive action programs are being overloaded with "nits" that are not system problems and their correction will not improve the system or provide any benefit to the organization. The Audit Function Improvement Process is an effective alternative for "short circuited" or overloaded corrective action programs. Yet, this process will provide more than just short-term relief. It also provides a mechanism for your organization to benefit from the audit process.

In this chapter we have addressed the initial part of this process. We have stressed the need to evaluate actions, to thoroughly assess the importance to the organization prior to developing the action plan. Included in this evaluation process is:

- An understanding that a finding or a problem can be a symptom, not the systematic problem that needs to be corrected
- An evaluation of the process and system before initiating action
- The gathering, correlation, and analysis of data
- A definition of the problem to be corrected
- Conferring with the auditor as appropriate

This filter, or evaluation, process is vital to the success of the Audit Function Improvement Process. Without investing the time to understand the system deficiencies, any actions taken will have no value for the organization and will be meaningless. On the other hand, when this evaluation is done effectively, the information generated will prove beneficial when developing the action plan. The action plan will be effective when the root cause for each finding has been identified. The corrective action teams are then able to determine alternative actions, which will guide the development of a complete action plan.

As the team continues through this Audit Function Improvement Process, they will provide information in the form of updates to the auditor who may provide valuable input through additional evaluation and "filtering" of information.

The value of the team's records is recognized when the team must re-evaluate actions or decisions made earlier in this process. These records may prove the auditor's or the team's viewpoint, but, in either case, they will save the team valuable time in resolving concerns. They will also prove to be a valuable asset when the team develops their plan for standardizing improvement actions, as we will see in the next chapter.

Chapter 6

Did It Work?

After trying out your plan of action for a while, you need to look at any changes that have happened. If you have been collecting information, you need to look at it and see if the problem has gotten better or has been solved. If you have not been gathering information, you need to do this now so that you can decide if the changes you made helped the situation.

Author: Matt Helderman, 9 years old
Our Steps to Quality, Koalaty Kid Program
Western Salisbury School, Allentown, PA

The wisdom of the above statement is very obvious. Has it gotten better? That is the point of it all. You did all this work and has the work been fruitful? Has it fixed the problem? Fixing the problem means the changes were effective.

The Corrective Action Must Be Effective

The meaning of effective is complex and subject to individual perceptions based on each person's own experiences. How effectiveness is verified is also variable. Some simply choose to ignore the true meaning of effectiveness, while others claim they do, but don't. There are major differences between how effectiveness is assessed between first-, second-, and third-party audits. The differences will be discussed later in this chapter. We will

111

start with requirements for effectiveness and their interpretation. The ISO standards and handbook text give us the following guidance:

- Auditors should determine the effectiveness of the implemented quality system in meeting specified quality objectives (ISO 10011-1-1994, clause 4.1).[13]

- To implement the quality management system, the organization shall: c) determine criteria and methods required to ensure the **effective** operation and control of these processes; (ISO/DIS 9001:2000, 4.1)[14]

- Top management shall review the quality management system, at planned intervals, to ensure its continuing suitability, adequacy and **effectiveness.** (ISO/DIS 9001:2000, 5.6.1)[15]

- The organization shall conduct periodic internal audits to determine whether the quality management system: b) has been **effectively** implemented and maintained. (ISO/DIS 9001:2000, 8.2.2)[16]

- The organization shall collect and analyze appropriate data to determine the suitability and **effectiveness** of the quality management system and to identify improvements that can be made. (ISO/DIS 9001:2000, 8.4)[17]

- According to the definition of a quality audit, an auditor has to determine whether quality activities and related results comply with planned arrangements and whether these arrangements are implemented effectively and are suitable to achieve objectives.[18]

The dictionary defines effective as: producing a decided, decisive, or desired effect (syn effect: consequence, result, event, issue, outcome).

People are still struggling with the idea of effectiveness because until after the first edition of this book was published, there wasn't much help in any of the standards and the dictionary uses abstract terms that could be interpreted several ways. We do know that whatever we do, we want it to work and for the boss to be pleased. There is no interest in implementing a solution that is going to double operating costs if there are no corresponding organizational benefits.

An insight about effectiveness is found in Stephen R. Covey's book, *The 7 Habits of Highly Effective People.* Here he states that effectiveness lies in the balance between production of desired results and production capability, which is the ability of an asset to produce a desired result.[19] Covey applies effectiveness to individual behavior, but the same concepts are true for organizations.

The Institute of Internal Auditors describes effectiveness using two terms: effective control and efficient performance.

> *Effective Control* is present when management directs events in such a manner as to provide assurance that the organization's objectives and goals will be achieved. *Efficient Performance* accomplishes objectives and goals in an accurate and timely fashion with minimal use of resources.[20] This provides additional insight, but be very careful of the use of the phrase, 'minimal use of resources.' The use of the word minimal can be easily abused by cost cutters. We prefer the phrase, *optimal* use of resources.

If the objectives and goals of an organization include requirements for accuracy, timelines, and the use of minimal resources, then efficient performance could be a subset of effective control.

In the Audit Function Improvement Process model, effectiveness should be checked at two points in the evolution of a solution. Effectiveness needs to be checked after testing a solution (try out the idea) and when the solution is implemented systemwide. It is always advisable to evaluate the effectiveness of a proposed corrective/preventive action, even for low-risk changes. If a small-scale test or model is developed, the data from the implementation of the test should be evaluated to determine if the solution was effective. There is considerable disagreement on the amount of testing and evaluation necessary prior to systemwide implementation of changes to the system. We can agree, however, that it is important to test corrective actions prior to full-scale implementation (it lowers the risk to the organization), and we can agree that the changes must be effective.

Therefore, the effectiveness of the solution (the corrective action) should be checked prior to full-scale implementation and again after the full-scale implementation (standardizing the improvement) stage.

Effective Means It Works

As an internal quality auditor, member of a corrective action team, audit program manager, or member of management, you may be assigned to assess a system change as a result of a corrective/preventive action. You will need to check the effectiveness of the change to determine if there are long-term beneficial results. If you are a stakeholder (process owner) it would be advisable to verify that corrective/preventive action has been implemented and is effective before the auditor arrives.

In the previous section, there is a reference to "effectively implemented." However, determining whether an action is effectively implemented and assessing whether a corrective action is effective are two different things (was it implemented and does it work).

Effectiveness of a corrective/preventive action has two components: (A) is it achieving the desired result? (Has the output improved? Is it consistent with organizational objectives?), and (B) is the process capable, efficient, and consistent with objectives? (Is the process designed to consistently achieve the required output? Is the process cost-effective?)

The components are further described as follows.

Component A—Effectively achieves the desired result (product/ output): There should be tangible results and the deliverable should provide added value. You can show improvement and that the problem was fixed. This is more than simply verifying that people did what they said they were going to do because you've got to collect data. The data may be that late delivery complaints have been eliminated, contaminated product has been cut by 50 percent, scrap reduced by 30 percent, etc. If you didn't achieve the desired result (improvement), you probably did not address the root cause (or all of the significant root causes) that contributed to the problem.

Component B—Effectively works (process): The process is capable and is efficient. The tangible results are produced from a process that is capable of doing it right all the time and is in concert with organizational objectives. In many cases an equilibrium must be reached between achieving the desired output and maintaining a capable efficient process. We could fix a problem by doubling the inspection to reduce shipment of contaminated product but it would not be cost effective (which is contrary to organizational objectives). This component of effectiveness is the most difficult to assess and may require a judgment from the person(s) evaluating the effectiveness of the change. The person needs to know and understand the organizational objectives and possess the knowledge and skills to determine if a process is capable and efficient. The person needs to know what process capability means, how to flowchart, and possibly have knowledge of statistical tools to evaluate data. It is unlikely that third-party auditors will have the necessary knowledge of the organization being audited and skills necessary to determine that the solution works effectively. In fact, some third-party organizations rotate their auditors every so many audits to maintain the auditors' objectivity. Rotating auditors is a good practice, but it prevents third-party auditors from fully understanding the auditee's organizational culture and objectives. However, it is likely that first-party auditors, process owners, corrective team members, and managment will (or should) possess the knowledge and skills necessary to determine that solutions work and are effective.

Not finding the equilibrium between components A and B is the root of management's reluctance to implement continuous quality improvement. Management wants improved results, but not at the expense of losing their business. It is unfortunate that in the past many quality professionals oversimplified the situation by pointing out that quality could be improved if the output (production) rate was reduced. The standard view was that poor quality was production's fault because of trying to produce too much, too fast. Management still fears that the abuse of quality principles will increase organizational costs. Figure 6.1 illustrates the balance between product/service targets and process capability.

An analogy would be: Effectiveness involves more than following standards and procedures for planting a crop and measuring the harvest. Effectiveness requires looking at how the soil or base fertility is maintained and how the seeds are prepared and stored. The land must be cared for and nurtured. Short-term, low-cost, high yields are achievable, but benefits cannot be sustained in the long term if soil is not nurtured and cared for and the seed stock is not continuously improved. You may have overheard farmers refer to low-yield farms or land as being "played out."

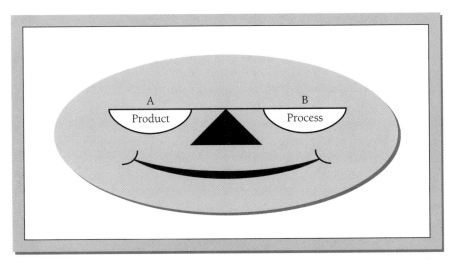

Figure 6.1. Product vs. process effectiveness balance.

Verifying effectiveness ensures that your organization does not find itself in the same condition—"played out."

Now we come to some newer definitions and additional guidance:

Effectiveness: the degree to which objectives are achieved in an efficient and economical manner. (*The Quality Audit Handbook,* 1999, page 113)

Effectiveness: measure of the extent to which planned activities are realized and planned results are achieved. (ISO/DIS 9000, 1999)

So there appears to be agreement that for something to be effective we must consider two components: achieving the desired results (the product) and how they were achieved (the process).

Unfortunately real determination of effectiveness is missing from most audit (or improvement) programs because it requires collecting data and a knowledge of the process as well as an understanding of organizational objectives.

All "effectiveness verifications" of changes to the system should include the evaluation of both conditions (product and process) to verify the effectiveness of a solution. It should be mandatory for internal audits and for self-verification by process owners. For second- (assessing suppliers) and third-party (independent body) auditors, the scope of the effectiveness verification will depend on the purpose and cost/benefit of the activity: cost because it will take time to collect and analyze data, and benefit because the auditor's ability to determine if a corrective action is effective is directly related to the person's work experience and skill base.

The prime directive for a third-party auditor is to verify that an organization has an established quality system that is in compliance with a requirements standard. The third-party organization is certifying that the audited organization is in compliance with the requirements in the quality systems standard. This is their number one job and both supplier and customer organizations depend on it. It is not likely that an external auditor (third party) would be privy to sufficient information to determine the total effectiveness of a system or process.

There are some things that can be done by second- and third-party auditors to evaluate the total effectiveness of corrective actions. For example, during the follow-up of corrective actions, the auditor can determine if the stakeholder (owner of the problem) identified data that will be collected to verify that the desired result is achieved and that the process is capable. Third-party and second-party auditors can determine whether the organization is verifying the effectiveness of corrective actions.

Back in chapter 5, where the stakeholder is planning the correction of problems, it would make sense for the alternate solutions to be tested (compared) against the two components of effectiveness. It is possible for the stakeholder to propose solutions that will eliminate the problem (preventing recurrence and occurrence), yet the actions taken may not be effective. The change to the process may cause other problems and result in less satisfactory output (product or service), or the proposed change could increase costs and reduce success rates. In one case, an organization added an ingredient to its product to improve dispersion, but an extra manufacturing step was added and the cost of the ingredient was very high. The solution improved product performance, but the profit margin was significantly reduced because the market was not willing to pay more for the improvement.

Effectively Implemented

Effectively implemented is commonly interpreted as: a system is defined and people are doing what is documented. This view is self-serving for both the auditor and process owner because it requires the least amount of information to confirm and is easy to do. The problem is that the organization is being lead astray from its primary goals of being competitive and satisfying the customer. This type of limited effectiveness verification may result in a system that does not deliver an acceptable product or service and a system (process) that is not capable and efficient enough to be competitive in the marketplace. The only consolation is that all the paperwork is in order.

For effective implementation, one should verify that people did what they said they were going to do and that everyone involved in the change is informed (educated). Informed could mean a discussion, training session, memorandum, or other means. This is important for a new process, process changes, or personnel changes (for example, the procedure was changed, the new equipment was installed, the specifications were changed).

Follow-Up Checks

Chapter 1, Case 1 reported a finding that material is not adequately identified to ensure that only materials meeting customers' requirements are used. The team took into account both achieving the desired goal and ensuring that the new process was capable.

In the chapter 3 vernier calipers example, a person checking out the corrective action for effectiveness would determine the following:

Q: Were the changes effectively implemented?

A: This was a team effort, changes were discussed with all machinists, and a new procedure was issued.

Q: Is the desired result (goals, targets) achieved?

A: The change was to standardize the current practice and to be clear on the use of vernier calipers. The process monitoring showed that the organization continues to meet targets as before the normalization of the procedure: 99.2% defect free.

Q: Is the changed process capable?

A: The overall process was never changed, just formalized. Monitoring results shows that the process continues to operated as before and is more consistent since the procedure was issued. The normalization of the procedure has not slowed production or led to administrative problems.

The following checklist could be used to verify that the corrective/preventive action was effectively implemented and that it was effective.

Effectiveness Checklist

Effectively Implemented (Deployed)?

R1: Were operating personnel made aware of the change and the purpose of the change?

R2: Did the organization consider what would be required to implement the change such as classroom training, on-the-job training, examples, new standards, directives issued, operator surveys, etc.?

R3: Were all relevant documents, system requirements, and record keeping requirements modified to reflect the change to the process/system?

Instructions?

Bill of materials?

Formulations?

Testing and inspection?

Specification, design?

Packaging and markings?

New purchased materials?

Product storage?

Service procedures?

R4: Is the person or function responsible for authorization of process changes clearly designated?

R5: If the product or service provided to the customer is affected, was the customer notified of the change?

R6: Is the change being followed consistently?

Effective Corrective/Preventive Action?

R1: Were output measures identified to monitor and verify that the process is achieving the desired result?

R2: Have desired expectations (outputs) been defined? Are outputs consistent with expectations?

R3: Were process measures identified to monitor and verify that the process/system is capable?

R4: Have desired expectations (process) been defined? Are process measures consistent with expectations?

R5: Are there records of the results?

R6: Is an emergency change procedure in place to prevent nonconforming product or service if the change is not working?

Auditor/Client Interface

The client/auditor can interface with the stakeholder (improvement team) at the verification of the effectiveness of the proposed corrective/preventive action (Figure 6.2, Step 11). Step 11 is for the stakeholder to verify that the proposed corrective action will be effective based on the data collected from the test or try out of the idea. When the auditor and stakeholder are communicating (for example, sharing monitoring results), ongoing advice about the effectiveness of the corrective/preventive action may be given. As an advisor, however, the auditor/client can verify if everything is on track or point out issues that may not have been addressed by the stakeholder (improvement team). It should not be forgotten that the auditor is also the originator of the problem identification. As the originator, the auditor (client, audit program manager) is one of the customers of the corrective action process.

For first-party audits (internal audits), there is no reason why the auditor (audit program representative) could not provide advice and input based on the data collected during monitoring. For second- and third-party situations, this interface is more difficult to formalize without the auditor (audit program representative) taking ownership of the problem and later the stakeholder telling the auditor, "I did what you told us to,

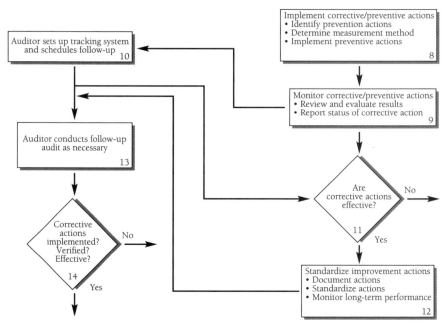

Figure 6.2. AFIP, step 8–14.

but of course it didn't work. It was a bad idea." The reality is that auditees frequently seek advice from auditors, but usually it is done informally and is therefore not binding on the auditee. In all audit situations, an auditor (audit program representative) should never make suggestions on how to solve a problem or handle a situation if the auditee is not fully aware that the advice is not binding—and may be wrong.

However, at Step 11 (Figure 6.2), you (the stakeholder) should not ask the auditor (audit program representative) how to fix anything, only to review and comment on the data collected from monitoring the results of the corrective action. The auditor should determine if the data verify that the proposed corrective action will effectively address the stated finding (problem). When the auditor limits comments to the facts, there won't be a problem. The review by the auditor can:

- Ensure that the problem-solving team is on track to solve the problem
- Be used by the auditor as data to justify closure of the corrective action
- Be used to schedule the final follow-up audit

- Give the problem-solving team a fresh view of the situation, another perspective that may turn up weaknesses not considered

Any allowed auditor and process owner interfaces occurring between the acknowledgment of the corrective/preventive action plan (Step 6) and final verification (Step 14) should be defined by the audit program manager. The audit program manager must decide if the interaction will add value or if the interaction will actually hinder improvement due to organizational culture.

Standardize Improvement Actions: Stakeholder

This is the actual implementation of the corrective/preventive action systemwide or processwide. You (the stakeholder) should apply the corrective action to all applicable lines, processes, services, products, hardware, and software. Applicable means the solution should be applied to all parts of the system that will eliminate the cause of the problem. This should be obvious to the stakeholder, depending on the nature of the corrective action. We will assume that you have the resources (capital and labor) to implement the corrective action.

Implementation of Systemwide Changes
Implementation of the corrective/preventive action should be considered on its own. Poor implementation of a good idea will still result in failure. Both implementation initiatives and timing are important factors for success.

During implementation you will be trying to influence people's behavior to be consistent with the new expectations. Managers use six basic techniques to influence behavior:

1. Issuing directives (orders)
2. Training
3. Planning (determining methods)
4. Inducements (such as monetary compensation)
5. Feedback from measures
6. Providing resources (people, financial, technology, etc.)

These techniques are in no particular order. The use of tying incentives to desired performance will not be discussed here. Using compensation levels to influence behavior assumes rational thinking (that is, people will change their behavior to maximize their wealth). Using compensation to motivate people has had mixed reviews over the last century, which is probably an indication that people are not always rational and that Hertzberg, a well-known behavioral scientist, was correct in saying that compensation is not a satisfier, it can only be a dissatisfier. Companies employ a number of other inducements to influence behavior such as outstanding work environments, awards, recognition, promise of promotions, warnings, or threat of termination.

The first step in implementation is to let people know about the change. This can be done verbally as well as with documents such as: directives, orders, standards, procedures, instructions, specifications, checklists, etc. All existing relevant documents should reflect the change, and there may be notification of the changed documents.

Next, training should be considered an integral part of the implementation process. Issuing orders in the private sector just doesn't have the same impact as in the military. In the military, orders are not supposed to be questioned. If directives (orders) aren't followed in industry, people can say they didn't know about it or they forgot. Training can be anything from five minutes of On-the-Job-Training with the boss to formal classroom presentations. Training may include live presentations, web based training (WBT), watching training videos, and observing examples of the procedure. The timing of training is very important. For training to be effective, it should be given around the same time the change (or new behavior) is expected. The training video and WBT mediums have the advantage of being available upon demand or when there is a need.

Plans should be issued for major changes that involve new processes or new products. These plans will detail the step-by-step implementation with milestones, coordination of interfaces, Gantt charts, and checks to make along the way. Implementation (project) plans should be issued for significant changes. Plans should include resource needs for people (number, skills, experience, knowledge), equipment, and technology.

Finally, you (the stakeholder or improvement team) can define output performance measures to take to provide feedback for trial-and-error adjustments. The feedback will influence process owner behavior to achieve satisfactory performance. Feedback measures come from monitoring long-term performance, which we cover in the next section.

These remarks are intentionally brief because change implementation is not our focus in this book; adequate references are available on the topic.

Monitor Long-Term Performance: Stakeholder

So far, so good. You decided what to do and you did it. Now comes the most important step in the improvement process (see Figure 6.2, Step 14)—did it work? The question means: Did it achieve the desired result? Is it consistent with organizational objectives? Is it efficient? Is it capable?

As soon as the change is made to the process (for example, reactor temperature increased, specifications changed, new start-up routine begun, method for taking orders changed), start monitoring the process. Monitoring includes collecting data to verify that the change is working and to measure possible effects on other processes or the system as a whole. How to monitor change is determined on a case-by-case basis as identified in the planning stages. However, as you learn more about the change (and you always do), what you need to monitor may change. Monitoring may require collecting new data in the short term, or closely monitoring the existing data more frequently.

The methods for monitoring can include one or more of the following:

1. Collecting new raw data from the process (a dimension, a test result).

2. Conducting process audits (short audits of just the process).

3. Monitoring existing data more frequently (special reports).

4. Using statistical techniques such as SPC (verify effect of change on process capability for specified parameter(s)).

5. Analyzing and trending raw data (trend charts, Pareto charts).

6. Comparing business performance data (organizational) to objectives (targets), percent improvement.

7. Analyzing and trending product performance data compared to desirable performance in a certain application. The key word here is *performance* compared to *specifications*. In many cases, the customer could care less about specifications as long as the product/service consistently provides the expected performance.

8. Using check sheets (maybe as part of a process audit).

9. Issuing and analyzing survey forms (for some of the more subjective changes). Has the customer's perception of the product luster improved? Do customers perceive that they are getting good, responsive service?

Collecting data is worthless unless someone looks at the data to verify that things are going as planned and, if not, tells someone so that adjustments can be made. An individual or team should be assigned the responsibility to watch the changes.

Even when you did a careful job in determining what parameters to monitor, it may be wrong because you can't keep everything else constant. Other components of the system/process are constantly changing and improving as well. A change in another part of the process could overshadow the results of the process changes you made. People need to monitor the data and filter out the unwanted and, when necessary, be prepared to change what is being monitored or where it is being monitored. For example, you may have taken steps to reduce complaints, but complaints increased because (unknown to you) six new products were introduced at the same time you started collecting data. Or you took steps to improve the part hardness at the same time that the material supplier changed its process and your data show no net improvement.

This monitoring step does not require many resources or much time, as depicted in our time-based PDCA diagram (refer to Figure 3.2). However, depending on what type of change was made, the length of time required for monitoring may be as long as a year.

Data Collection

Data can come from walking out to the shop floor and looking at a gauge once a week or from sophisticated monitoring equipment that sends data to a computer that generates reports—it can be simple or it can be complicated. The rule here is to keep it as simple as possible. Face it, this is an inspection step and does not deserve any more resources than absolutely necessary. If you did your homework, the data will quickly verify that the corrective action worked. The cycle time should also be designed to be short whenever possible.

There's a saying that for every action there is a reaction. Simply, if a change is made to a process it is likely (count on it) that something else is going to be affected. That something else is probably bad; it is probably undesirable. These side effects can include reduced capacity, another product property going haywire, slower output, increased costs, etc. Be sure to consider potential side effects of the process change before starting to monitor them. Sources of data are:

1. Collect raw data. First, identify a parameter that will indicate that the change is in control and working, such as a pressure reading, temperature, a test result, or physical count. Most of the

time, raw data are collected and charted or incorporated into a table by date, by machine, by line, by area, and so on.

If your problem is that reactor temperature instructions are not consistent and operators were not following the instructions, data collection might involve checking the daily data log and comparing it to the specified operating temperature.

If the problem is the number of orders that change, the raw data might look like the following:

	February	March	April	May	June	July
Orders changed	42	38	42	47	43	48
Orders canceled	4	12	4	3	4	3

The data indicate that order changes are slowly increasing and the level of canceled orders was constant except in March.

2. Conduct process audits. Process audits examine the process as a whole. From time to time, audit the process relative to the changes by looking at people, equipment, materials, methods (procedures, instructions), tests (or measures), and the operating environment.

For example assume there was a finding for not maintaining the demagnetizer equipment, which resulted in higher metallic particle levels in the final product. The demagnetizer was in a remote area of the plant on the fourth floor. Work instructions required that the demagnetizer be checked weekly. This could be an ideal case for conducting monthly process audits to verify that the process (checking the cleaning process of the demagnetizer) is working.

3. Monitor the existing data more frequently with special reports. Find out what data are currently being recorded to avoid duplicate reporting. We have seen situations in which certain data were always collected but management stopped looking at it years ago.

If a quality cost system is in place, this is a good place to start looking for data that could be used to monitor improvement.

4. Use statistical techniques such as SPC to verify effect of change on process capability for a specified parameter(s).

5. Analyze and trend raw or calculated data (trend charts, Pareto charts). The bar chart in Figure 6.3 could indicate that change

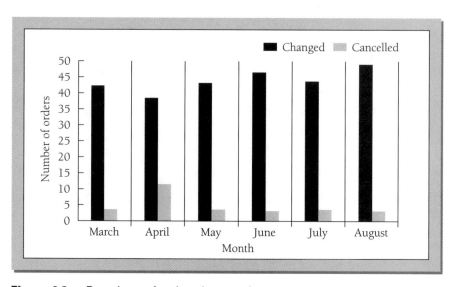

Figure 6.3. Bar chart of orders by month.

orders have been constant or increasing. Looking at changed orders as a percent of all orders received, however, may offer a different conclusion (see Figure 6.4).

The second graph shows that order changes decreased in July and August as a percent of all orders received. The selection of data to monitor is very important. If you select the wrong data, you could reach the wrong conclusion. Figure 6.4 is typical of an improvement curve: when you draw attention to a specific parameter or item, the number of incidents increases at first, then later you see the improvement. This phenomenon has always been difficult to explain; after all, numbers don't lie—or do they? In this case, if what constituted a change order was not clearly defined, there would be some ambiguity regarding when an order was a changed order and when it was a new order or a rescheduled order. The baseline data may change with the new definition and with managers bringing attention to the parameter as important to the organization.

6. Comparing business performance data to objectives. Organizations are driven largely by relative performance against competitors, against similar processes, or against other facilities (plant, line, office). Many goals and objectives are set with relative performance in mind, and many improvement programs

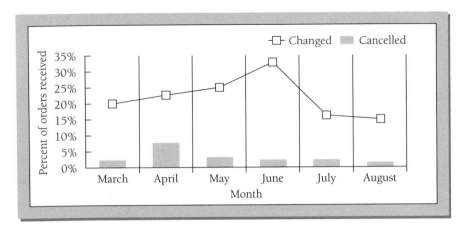

Figure 6.4. Bar chart of orders by percent per month.

are designed around relative performance (such as competitive benchmarking). You have probably heard the story about two campers that were being chased by a bear and one camper stopped to put on tennis shoes. The other camper asked why he stopped, and the reply was, "I don't need to outrun the bear. I just need to outrun you." And so goes the reality of business performance. Rarely do organizations set utopian quality goals (the brightest, strongest, fastest, biggest, or most consistent) unless they believe that they will benefit with increased profits or greater market share or reduced risk to the organization. Many of us in the quality field can embrace ideas such as narrowing process variation or increasing customer satisfaction as justifiable goals. But management doesn't accept these goals at face value unless they benefit the organization.

Management is a customer of the corrective/preventive action process and expects benefits. Monitoring changes (improvements) compared to business performance gets management's attention; comparison to business goals should be done when feasible. For example, for the change order problem, management might be interested in comparing the organization to similar organizations or comparing from plant to plant.

We should note that measurement of customer satisfaction is gaining wide acceptance in the quality management standards and business community as correlating to business performance. An index called the American Customer Satisfaction Index

(ACSI) has been developed by ASQ and the National Quality Research Center at the University of Michigan. The index was developed to provide a measure of quality and customer satisfaction to complement current measures of the U.S. economy. ACSI is based on evaluations of the quality of goods and services sold in the United States. The first ACSI was released in October 1994. An article in the ACSI Update newsletter indicates that it could prove to be advantageous to invest in companies that have a good ACSI (or other customer satisfaction) rating.[21]

7. Analyze and trend performance data. Regardless of the product or service specifications, customers may only be interested in how the product performs, how it looks, or the outcome of performed service. Many companies do not have specifications to guarantee that the product will perform as intended, so they develop performance tests as a check. Product test examples could include testing powder solubility, "hand" for fabrics, grinding efficiency, ease of maintaining, durability and reliability, that the equipment (engine) starts, and so on. One manufacturer of complex machinery conducts a try-out of all equipment. A product is not shipped unless it passes the try-out test. Even though the company has thousands of part specifications with hundreds of monitored processes, personnel still try it out to be sure that all the parts, when assembled, do what they are supposed to do. A service organization may have developed a new, more accurate process for registering students, but if it takes twice as long and overloads the telephone system it will not be effective.

8. Use check sheets (maybe as part of a process audit). A check sheet is used to record frequency of events, numbers, results, verifications, and so on. In the change order example given, a clerk could fill in a check sheet each month to record change order reasons (see Table 6.1).

9. Issue and analyze customer survey forms. Customer perception, regardless of the improvement made, may be all that matters. For product companies, surveys could include subjective measures such as color, luster, richness, solid feel, ease of use, and so on. Surveys for service companies can include asking about what was learned in class, completeness and accuracy of responses, availability of information, professionalism,

Reason for order changes	February	March
Wrong product identification/ model number	✓✓✓✓ ✓✓✓✓	✓✓✓✓ ✓✓✓
Product not in inventory as stated	✓✓✓	✓✓
Customer needs different product	✓✓	✓
Canceled order/duplicate order	✓✓✓	✓✓✓✓ ✓✓✓✓ ✓✓
Wrong quantity	✓✓✓✓ ✓✓	✓✓✓✓
Change delivery time/date/mode	✓✓✓✓ ✓✓✓✓ ✓✓✓✓	✓✓✓✓ ✓✓✓✓ ✓✓✓✓
Product not in specification	✓	✓✓
Change container/packaging	✓✓	✓
Change special instructions	✓	✓✓
Total	46	50

Table 6.1. Check sheet of reasons for order changes.

thoroughness, perceived value of the service, perceived courtesy, and so on.

The data to be collected must be determined by the process owner (stakeholder). It could be any of the above or a combination thereof. Whatever is measured, it must properly measure the effect of the change (improvement). In one case, the distribution department was doing a stellar job improving their operation, so management asked for a report of the distribution complaints over the last nine months. The raw data indicated that complaints had steadily increased. This surprise result disappointed upper management, the distribution department was not recognized for their improvement efforts, and the department manager was replaced several months later. The data did not reflect the acquisition of a new business, three new product lines, and changing to a higher-quality carrier that was more conscientous about reporting problems.

Let the Auditor Organization Know What's Happening

The process owner (stakeholder) can keep the auditor organization (or client) informed of progress toward full-scale implementation and the data collected after implementation. The auditor organization (or client) uses the data to determine if a follow-up audit is needed or if the corrective action can be closed based on existing data.

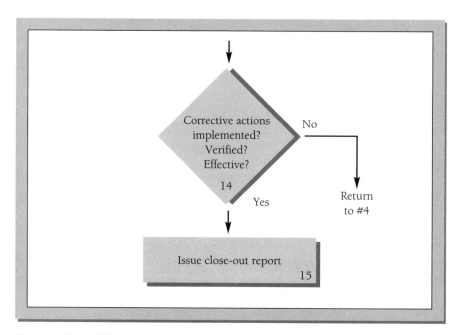

Figure 6.5.   AFIP, steps 14 and 15.

Follow-Up Activities

The purpose of a follow-up audit is to verify that the corrective action was implemented and that it was effective (Figure 6.5). This is one of the least-understood and least-utilized auditor activities. Plus, a follow-up audit takes on a very different tone between first-party, second-party, and third-party audits.

Good practice is that corrective actions should be followed-up by an independent party to verify that action has been taken. After verification, remove the corrective action from the to-do list (open corrective actions).

Follow-Up Internal Assessments

For internal audits (first party), management views follow-up audits as making sure people did what they said. Managers may perceive that a follow-up to corrective actions (Figure 6.5, Step 14) has little value, and it ends up having a low priority. It is not unusual for follow-up audits to be on the bottom of the to-do list.

Follow-up audits provide an independent view of the effectiveness of the corrective action. This can be valuable if the problem solvers miss the mark because they only took remedial action or they were not able to identify the root cause. If the follow-up is viewed as a partnership activity between the auditor organization and the stakeholder (two heads are better than one), this changes the perspective. Two reasonable people should be able to conclude whether the corrective action was implemented and effective. After all, if the corrective action was not implemented as promised, it is typically a priority issue that management controls. If the corrective action only addressed the symptoms and not the root cause, there may be a problem with the corrective action process itself or simply lack of knowledge and understanding by the problem solvers. In any case, if the problem was not fixed, not only is the organization not getting the benefits of the corrective action, but resources have been expended with no value added. This is important information for management to have.

You can view the follow-up as the final exam. If you pass, it is a simple matter to report that it works! If you fail, go back and find out the true root cause or causes and then correct it. This is where the stakeholder may have a problem. If the management culture is to penalize people for failure, it is natural for the stakeholder to avoid a follow-up audit.

It is said that you cannot succeed unless you are willing to fail. To succeed, you need to take calculated risks, which means you will fail once in a while. To avoid all risk is to do nothing, which is contrary to the best interests of the organization. So, it is in the best interests of the organization for management not to place individual blame for failure to address the root cause. If failing to identify the underlying cause is a common occurrence, management should be concerned about corrective action process effectiveness, not individual performance.

Follow-Up Second- and Third-Party Audits

Follow-up activities from outside organizations (customer or independent registration/certification authority) take on an entirely different personality than internal audit follow-ups. Second- and third-party audits are normally done under a contract. There is a contractual relationship outlining the obligations of both parties. Thus, correcting the problems found in second-and third-party audits is not optional. For second- party audits, failure to correct problems could result in loss of business, and for third-party audits it could result in loss of certification (quality system registration/certification, product certification) or endorsement of the organization or product. Because of the commitment of the organization (the contract), follow-up to corrective action becomes a very serious matter.

We encourage second- and third-party auditors not to overreact if they find that a corrective action has not been implemented or is not effective. It could be that important business matters had to be addressed first, or it could have been an honest oversight. True, the excuse that an important business matter had to be addressed first is overused, but it doesn't make it any less true. After all, the organization has a business to run. If failure to address corrective actions happens time and time again, there is cause for concern and a finding should be issued based on the record of repeat occurrences.

Realities of Follow-Up Audits

Follow-up audits take time and resources. We suggest that there are alternatives to special follow-up audits. First, corrective actions can be followed up during regularly scheduled audits of the area. The lead auditor or client only needs to include the verification of corrective actions in the purpose statement and secure a list of open corrective actions from the auditee or client.

Second, if the audit team has been working in partnership with the stakeholder (improvement team) and receiving data from the testing and implementation of the corrective action, the data could serve as verification that the corrective action was implemented and effective.

Some practitioners suggest that corrective actions can be closed out prior to actual systemwide implementation of the actions. While this is contrary to good audit practices, business realities may make this an attractive option. For most organizations undertaking a major change that represents a high risk, some type of prototype testing or modeling is included in the implementation. This is typical of changes that require capital funds, but is not limited to capital projects. If the data from monitoring the test verifies that the corrective action is effective and management has approved its implementation systemwide (approved the capital project request, or included it in business plan changes) why not issue the audit close-out report? The reality is that once a corrective action has been verified as effective after the try-out step (Figure 6.2, Step 11), 99 percent of the time the organization will move forward with its full-scale implementation. The remaining 1 percent of the time, management may delay or cancel the implementation for business reasons (dropped the product line, selling the business, changing the market strategy, etc.), which is also justifiable. Therefore, for practical reasons, it may be more appropriate to close out the audit finding after verification of the tested corrective action (the individual CAR) than to keep it open for the next year or two until the new equipment is installed and operating. If corrective actions are closed based on test results, an audit of close-outs should be scheduled every one to three years to ensure that there are no problems with this approach (that is, closing out corrective action prior to systemwide implementation).

Chronic Unresponsiveness

You will need to be prepared for lack of responsiveness on the part of the auditee despite your best efforts. You should always keep accurate records to measure progress and provide creditable information concerning follow-up activities. You should always be fair, objective and give people the benefit of the doubt. When developing your procedures be sure to include what should be done when the auditee is unresponsive to corrective action requests or when investigations always result in superficial responses. Some possible actions to chronic unresponsiveness could be:

- Remain positive and meet with auditee to determine reason(s) and issue a joint plan for improvement.
- The third time the target date is changed: issue another nonconformance, for not responding to the corrective action request. This will lead to an investigation to identify system concerns and improvement areas (the three strikes rule).
- Forward information to the assigned person's supervisor as input for performance review.
- Meet with assigned person's supervisor to discuss establishing an individual performance goal for responding to corrective action requests.
- Inform others of the risk of an external audit nonconformity on the corrective action process.

Close-Out Report

The deliverable of the follow-up process is a brief report (Step 15) that states the audit item (problem item) is either still open or that it is closed. To close out a finding means that the corrective/preventive action has addressed the problem, is implemented, and is effective. It is convenient to include a section on the CAR form (see Figure 6.6) to record that the corrective action was followed-up and verified.

Were There Benefits? Time to Celebrate!

When all is said and done, you are not really done yet. You have determined the root cause of the problem, implemented a change to eliminate the cause, and checked it to ensure that you got the desired result. Next, you need to determine the benefit to the organization. Determining benefits is most effective when quantified in dollars. Money is the universal

CORRECTIVE ACTION REQUEST	
Date: 25 May 20XX	CAR number: 950525-03

Auditee: Our Company Ourtown, MI	Audit number: 950525

Finding:
Products and materials are not adequately identified to ensure that only materials meeting the customers' requirements are used.

Contact	Auditor
Signature: *John B. Brannick*	Signature: *James D. Hillside*
Title: *Material Contract Mgr.*	Title: *Lead Auditor*

Remedial Action:
1. Segregate all unidentified products and raw materials.
2. Set up reevaluation process for all such materials prior to use.

Root Cause: Conflicting procedures: purchasing, control of non-conforming product, raw material control, and process test procedures.

Corrective Action Plan (to prevent recurrence):
1. Reevaluate processes involved to ensure that requirements are understood.
2. Revise each of the procedures involved.
3. Include purchasing, engineering, manufacturing, and quality departments on future document reviews.

Corrective Action Plan Dates: Start June 5, 20XX   Complete July 30, 20XX   Auditor Acceptance: Date:

Corrective Action Taken (to prevent recurrence):
1. Revised procedures
2. Train departments on new methods
3. Conducted four process audits to verify effectiveness. No major problems.
4. Standardized to all applicable areas.
5. Scrap reduced by 70 percent and no customer complaints reported during the test period.

Signature: *John B. Brannick*   Date: August 7, 20XX

Corrective Action Approved [X]   Corrective Action Disapproved [ ]   Auditor: *James D. Hillside*

Follow-Up Audit Date: September 29, 20XX   Signature: *James D. Hillside*

Close-Out Date: October 3, 20XX   Signature: *James D. Hillside*

Figure 6.6. Completed CAR.

yardstick. Here, quality professionals are often out of their area of expertise, but shouldn't be. Every important thing an organization does must relate to its organizational benefit except the nondiscretionary activities required by regulations. This is true for all commercial organizations and should be true for all organizations, although public sector organizations struggle with this idea since they are not profit seeking. The lack of focus on efficiency in the public sector has resulted in dollars used in very ineffective and inefficient ways. For example, the U.S. government disaster relief program does not expect to make a profit, but could focus on benefit (deliverable) versus cost. Determining the organizational benefits (improvement) applies to everyone.

Quality Costs

A tool to determine benefits is the use of a quality cost system. There are several good books published on the subject, and we recommend that anyone involved in the quality improvement process study how quality costs (or the cost of poor quality) can be used to assess the benefits of improvement efforts. Quality cost techniques attempt to capture both the apparent costs of failure and the hidden costs of failure. Hidden costs are typically several times larger than apparent costs. As discussed in chapter 2, however, quality cost systems have their limitations and could make reporting very complicated.

Organizational Costs (Business Costs)

Businesses and organizations use different sets of terminology than auditors. Operations and manufacturing groups think in terms of reducing costs and increasing output. They like to hear how costs were reduced that resulted in lower cost per unit, lower daily expenses, reduced working capital, lower capital expenditure requirements, and so on. The same data could be used to talk to the business and marketing folks in terms of profit margin, profit, return on sales, or return on equity. If these terms are unfamiliar to you, get some training to understand the terms and then start using them.

In the case of first-party audits, determining the benefits is important to show the contributions of the audit program and to get management support for it. Report the benefits to management and the team members. This is positive reinforcement that they are doing the right things.

For second-party audits, determining the benefits is important when a supplier-customer partnership program is in place. If the relationship with the supplier is purely contractual, then benefit calculations are of limited value and may not be worth the effort to calculate.

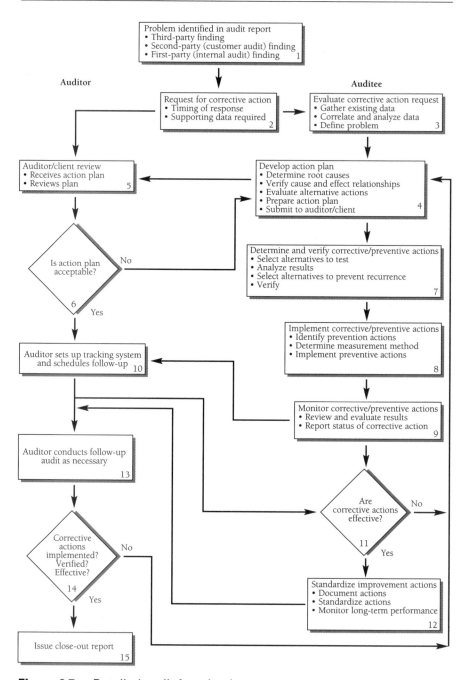

Auditor

Auditee

Problem identified in audit report
- Third-party finding
- Second-party (customer audit) finding
- First-party (internal audit) finding 1

Request for corrective action
- Timing of response
- Supporting data required 2

Evaluate corrective action request
- Gather existing data
- Correlate and analyze data
- Define problem 3

Auditor/client review
- Receives action plan
- Reviews plan 5

Develop action plan
- Determine root causes
- Verify cause and effect relationships
- Evaluate alternative actions
- Prepare action plan
- Submit to auditor/client 4

Is action plan acceptable? 6 — No

Yes

Determine and verify corrective/preventive actions
- Select alternatives to test
- Analyze results
- Select alternatives to prevent recurrence
- Verify 7

Implement corrective/preventive actions
- Identify prevention actions
- Determine measurement method
- Implement preventive actions 8

Auditor sets up tracking system and schedules follow-up 10

Monitor corrective/preventive actions
- Review and evaluate results
- Report status of corrective action 9

Auditor conducts follow-up audit as necessary 13

Are corrective actions effective? 11 — No

Yes

Corrective actions implemented? Verified? Effective? 14 — No

Yes

Standardize improvement actions
- Document actions
- Standardize actions
- Monitor long-term performance 12

Issue close-out report 15

Figure 6.7. Detailed audit function improvement process.

Celebrate!

Always take time to celebrate. This does not need to be a parade down Main Street. It can be as simple as a lunch or a meeting to recognize the efforts of the team with the boss in attendance. Celebrate small victories as well as big ones. Celebrating is an investment in solving future problems. The team's motivation to continue may depend on it.

Summary

This chapter dealt with following-up the implemented corrective/preventive action. We discussed how the audit program representative and stakeholder can verify that the cause of the problem was eliminated. We reviewed the multiple interfaces to show how to verify results with the optimal use of resources.

Implementation of corrective/preventive actions should be verified in the following ways:

- Check for effectiveness. Corrective/preventive actions should be verified that they were *effective,* meaning that the action achieves the desired result and the process is capable and efficient. An equilibrium must be achieved between output goals and the process that provides the output.

- Monitor corrective/preventive actions. It is not sufficient to implement a solution and walk away from it; this could do more harm than good. You must identify the measures that will be monitored to objectively verify that the corrective/preventive action worked.

- Follow-up. Auditors, when charged to do so, must verify the corrective/preventive action. Verification can be accomplished by a follow-up audit or by analyzing results (data). The verification must be recorded.

Now you have completed the detailed Audit Function Improvement Process flowchart that is shown in Figure 6.7.

Chapter 7

Effective Audit Program Management

The purpose of this chapter is to bring together everything discussed in the previous chapters under the management of the audit program. We discuss how to manage the audit service to maximize its contribution to the organization. All too frequently, audit program managers only report the number of audits and findings to gauge their performance. We introduce methods for setting management goals and objectives for the audit program and discuss what should be tracked and monitored. We will review opportunities for improvement of first-, second-, and third-party audit organizations. However, our primary focus is on internal audit programs because they have the greatest flexibility and can have the biggest effect on improvement (value-added service).

The internal audit function may be either a separate department of an organization with a staff of auditors or it may be one person in charge of auditing that borrows auditors from other departments as needed. The internal audit function should be managed like any other function within the organization (accounting, operations, sales and marketing, development, etc.). Historically, the audit function has been viewed as an internal police force (or worse, secret police). The audit function was further isolated from other management functions because upper management thought outputs (reports) would be biased unless total independence was maintained. Separating the audit function from other management functions has kept managers from realizing its full potential in terms of good management practices and techniques. We maintain that the audit function of an organization should not be treated differently from other functions/departments and that it should be accountable for its performance.

Auditing Service

The audit function provides a service to the organization just like the accounting or purchasing departments. A quality audit (assessment) is a personalized service. The customer (the auditee, the organization and the client) is purchasing the skills and knowledge of the auditors to conduct a professional audit of the customer's process or system and prepare a report on what they found. For second- and third-party audits there is usually a contract and an agreed-upon fee. For internal first-party audits, money rarely changes hands, but internal funds may transfer to the audit function. An internal chargeback system to pay for internal audits would be a way to monitor performance and indicate the need (contribution) for the audit function. The internal customer will usually contract to use the service (the audit plan) for a specified time in a specified area. The only tangible product is the audit report.

As the audit service supplier, the audit function employs auditors with skills (interviewing, report writing, investigating, data analysis) and knowledge of performance standards and audit conventions. In most cases, customers do not have the skills or specific knowledge to do it themselves, and even if they did, an internal self-audit is less effective because auditors from the same function/department would not be independent of the organization/department being audited. We have seen internal self-audits work okay the first time, a little less effectively the second time, and be a completely wasted effort each succeeding time. Bias creeps in and the auditors start saying to themselves, "Why ask the question when I already know the answer?"

The customer—auditee, client, or organization—hopes to benefit from the audit service. Audits provide benefits to the customer through identification of the following:

- Areas to reduce costs, to help the organization stay competitive.

- Improvement opportunities—to be able to do more or sell more.

- Risks to the organization's wealth or well-being, such as through identifying regulatory noncompliances. (Note that third-party certification audits fall into this category.)

In the past, the audit service only focused on the risk issues related to legal compliance. It is important to avoid mandated regulatory enforcement and monetary penalties, but this limited output tends to put auditing in the cost-of-doing-business category. Managers want to see higher value-added outputs before they'll consider quality auditing an important management tool.

People are more critical of services and products than ever before. Organizations that provide an audit service need to be prepared to explain the benefits of the service.

Basic Audit Process Elements

Some believe that the audit program manager is only responsible for selecting and training auditors, scheduling audits, and ensuring that audits take place. What if the sales department manager stated that he or she is only responsible for selecting salespeople, training them, scheduling sales calls, and ensuring that the sales calls take place? We think the organization's top management would object to a scope of responsibilities that did not include such things as sales goals, increasing profit margin, and pricing structure.

All of the major quality performance standards (ISO 10011, ISO 19011, ISO 9004, and the Baldrige Award criteria) either require or suggest that the audit function should continually improve. To gain some insight into how to improve the audit program process, we will first review basic audit program management elements (historical) and then explore modern audit program elements (future expectations).

First, we need to explore the basic elements (Figure 7.1) that must be in place for a proper audit function to operate. We will use the fishbone diagram to describe the basic audit program elements (people, equipment, methods, measures, materials, and environment). You will need people and the people will need to know what to do.

People

The audit program manager must hire people to do the audits. They may either be full-time auditors or part-time auditors selected from other departments within the organization, or outside subcontractors. Organizations that conduct second-party or third-party audits typically hire or subcontract people to do the work.

The people you select must be qualified to do the work assigned. Qualification criteria should be defined and can include specific knowledge,

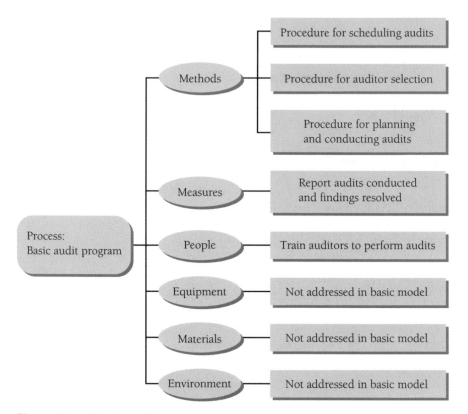

Figure 7.1. Basic audit program process.

experience, personal attributes, and skills. To be qualified, the auditor should be knowledgeable of quality system audit techniques and the performance standards that will be used in the audits (ISO 9001, QS-9000, Shingo Prize, President's Award, etc.). Internal auditors should take some type of basic audit training. Auditors should also receive training in how to interpret performance standards and learn through study and on-the-job training (working with qualified auditors). Third-party ISO 9001 audit organizations usually require their people to take an accredited five-day (36-hour) training course.

Methods

There should be a procedure for how to conduct an audit (that is, what you do before, during, and after the audit). The procedure should define how the qualifications of personnel conducting the audit (for example., relative experience, skills and/or knowledge) are determined.

There should be some type of defined rationale for developing audit schedules or audit program plans. The areas that can be audited should be defined. The reason for doing an audit can include a routine check, changes to the process, a new product or service, or reported problems.

Measures of Audit Function Performance

Typically, the two basic measures of audit function performance are the number of audits conducted and the number and status of findings. These measures have limited added value to upper management.

Modern Audit Process Elements

Implementing the basic audit program elements is not enough. The audit function will not be respected as a part of the management team if they only schedule and conduct audits. Scheduling audits and developing qualified auditors is only the start. We believe the audit department should be accountable for much more than this. Earlier we discussed the audit process as part of the management function and that management is a customer of the audit service. We think the audit program should have goals and performance targets like any other function. There should be methods to continuously improve the audit program through feedback and recommendations. The audit organization should report to management how the audit program is meeting customer (client, management, auditee) needs; this is true for first-, second-, and third-party auditor organizations. There should be plans for staffing, training, and operating, and key parameters for efficiency and productivity should be defined and monitored.

Key parameters should be monitored to ensure the success of the audit program. These could include audit cycle-time reporting and initiatives to reduce audit time, such as the use of notebook computers to reduce the report time. Measures could include numbers and types of audits, corrective actions completed, the effect corrective actions have on reducing the organization's cost of quality, and the results of auditing the auditors. Tips for monitoring performance could also be taken from service functions, since auditing is a service. Customer feedback in some form such as an evaluation or survey is appropriate. Most auditees (customers) would welcome the opportunity to evaluate the audit function! The key parameters monitored should tie into the organization's objectives (mission).

The culture of fear and mistrust that was created in the past may need a major remake. The audit function may be perceived as closed and almost secret. Managers in other departments may fear auditors and view them as nit-pickers that only care about meeting their quota of findings. The auditors will be more effective if they don't consider their job finished when they report a finding. After all, auditors are stakeholders in the improvement process too. Even if auditors do not participate in the follow-up and corrective action process, they should want to know if they are helping or hindering the organization.

When the audit function enjoys the same responsibility and accountability as other departments, it will be accepted as an important part of the organization.

Let's look at the process elements of a modern audit program using a cause-and-effect diagram (see Figure 7.2).

People

The people selected to perform internal quality system audits should be the organization's best people. Auditors can have a tremendous effect on the organization if audits are used as a management tool for improvement. Poor auditors can demoralize the organization and up-end the audit program. Outstanding performers will have a corresponding positive effect on the organization. We suggest that organizations consider an assignment as a quality system auditor to be part of the career path to upper management. A person's outstanding performance on the audit team will reach across departments and the individual will get a rare view of how the overall organization functions. Few people know as much about how an organization works as an auditor who has evaluated several functions. Senior management needs to appreciate the contribution the auditing experience can make to the organization.

Note: If in your heart you know that you have been assigned as an auditor because of not fitting in, this is your opportunity to turn things around and show your stuff. You have an ideal opportunity to add value to the organization, see different parts of the organization, and give presentations (visibility). In short, you have been handed a chance to be able to dazzle everyone with your ability and knowledge.

Getting the best people is also critical to third-party audit organizations. Some third-party organizations are better than others, but about 90 percent of their reputation rests on how auditors conduct themselves during the audit (examination) and the quality of the report.

Auditors should have a minimum level of work experience. For third-party registrars, this is automatically accomplished by only using certified auditors (RAB quality system auditors, IQA IRCA auditors). For first-party auditors, you should set some minimum work experience requirement.

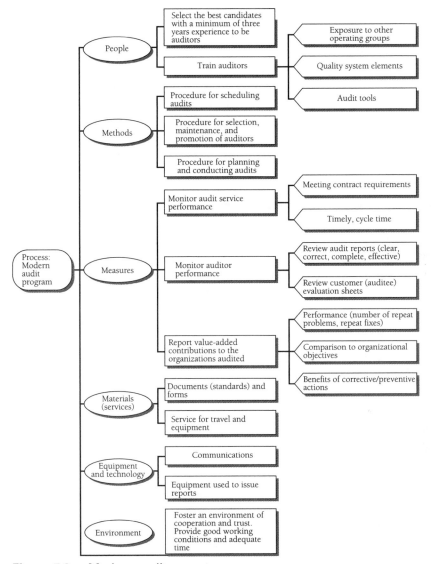

Figure 7.2. Modern audit program process.

We suggest a three-year minimum. New hires right out of school are not going to be good auditors as they are still trying to figure out what the work world is all about.

Education level is a different matter altogether. An auditor does not need to have a bachelor's degree in engineering or the sciences. We know many good auditors that have high school diplomas. Education level and type of education needed will depend on what is expected of the auditor. Auditors with a bachelor's degree are going to do a better job of auditing technical areas compared to someone with a hotel management degree. Someone with a motel management degree is going to do a better job of auditing a ready-to-use service organization (hotels, car rental, etc.).

Next, you will need an ongoing training program for new and experienced auditors. The training for new auditors should bring them up to speed with the audit process (most everyone is doing a fair job in this aspect of training). Training of new auditors and support staff should include awareness of fundamental quality management principles. Here, we assume that the audit function practices what it preaches and that some type of continuous improvement program and/or quality system is in place.

Training of existing auditors is necessary to sharpen their tool skills and knowledge so that they will continually add value to the audit process. Auditors should understand the use of statistical techniques such as the following:

- Pareto analysis
- Histograms
- Statistical process control
- Check sheets, checklists
- Cause-and-effect diagrams
- Sampling methods
- Flowcharts
- Trend charts
- Management tools, such as affinity diagrams, matrix diagrams, priorities matrix, tree diagrams
- Other techniques such as design of experiments (DOE), depending on organizational requirements

Auditors should understand total quality management and the fundamental elements of a quality system such as:

- The corrective/preventive action process
- Continuous improvment
- Customer satisfaction
- Configuration control
- The use of computers for documents and records

- Metrology
- Quality plans and strategic quality planning
- Project planning
- Problem-solving techniques (synetics)
- Cost of poor quality

Auditors should understand management lingo and universal financial terms. This is important (as explained in chapter 2) so that the auditor will know management's hot buttons and how to push them.

There is also a need to train auditors in functions they are not familiar with, such as exposing an engineer to how the purchasing and sales processes work, or exposing a purchasing agent to how a laboratory works. Thus, periodic tours of various departments should be included as part of the ongoing training program.

Additionally, auditor performance should be monitored to determine continued qualification. This can be done through customer feedback and comparison to performance measures.

Audit experience should only be one of the factors used to identify lead auditors and/or senior auditors (see the section on "Measures" dealing with audit evaluation feedback forms).

Methods

Organizations and departments need to establish methods for conducting their business. Methods (procedures) need to be communicated to those that will be using them. Many times methods are established to implement (deploy) a process and plan. The methods (rules, manuals, procedures, instructions) need to be written when they involve significant risk. By risk we mean the probability of any type of danger to the well-being of the organization such that it is necessary to strictly follow certain rules or defined processes, by the book, and failure to follow a prescribed method or rule will lead to significant problems. You should consider writing out the following documents as good practice.

- Defining the mission of the auditing function relative to the overall organizational mission
- Defining a process for the introduction of new audit services and changes to existing services (such as method of reporting or adding a new performance standard)
- Establishing a process for how audits should be conducted
- Providing examples and guidelines for reports

- Defining how documents and records will be handled and retained
- Establishing a training policy and associated procedures
- Defining auditor qualifications (certification) and the approval process
- Invoicing (pricing) or fund transfer methods

Measures

The measures used to monitor the performance of the audit function are a direct reflection of the audit program's purpose. The appropriate measures for a first-, second-, and third-party audit organization may be different, or various forms of the same performance parameters. We have divided our discussion in this section by type of audit; however, because of the overlap and the sidebar discussions, please read all the sections.

First Party. The audit manager needs to communicate to the audit team that the purpose of audits (assessments, examinations) is to help a given unit, division, or location to improve performance. The audit manager may then be able to effectively base the measures of audit program performance on that unit's goals. In other words, when the audit manager develops an audit program plan for the fiscal year, the manager must ensure that the audits assist the business unit to evaluate performance against business goals and the company's goals, or the audit program will not be successful.

The audit manager or other management personnel may also track the open corrective actions for each audit. The data provided with each demonstrate the improvement achieved by the customer (auditee). An effective method of evaluating the audit program is to plot the corrective action from the initial performance level (observed in the initial audit) through the corrective action process against the stated performance goal. The audit manager can expand and standardize comparison methods using measures that are meaningful to the audit customer and to the company as a whole. The closer the relationship of these measures to external customer needs and business goals, the more effective they will be.

SIDEBAR

No corrective action tracking and follow-up techniques will work unless top management supports the program. Top management should make it clear that corrective action is mandatory and continued lateness will not be tolerated.

Field experience for tracking corrective actions:

1. Conduct monthly staff meetings to review status of open corrective actions from audits and other sources. Department managers can explain overdue status (plan, trial, deploy, verify effectiveness) and commit to new dates. The top management person should attend.

2. Report progress of corrective actions on a common board or on the computer network that is highly visible to everyone.

3. The computer can be programmed to notify the auditor or management by the corrective action response date, trial date, and implementation date. Some organizations escalate the notification to the next level of management, when auditees are unresponsive.

4. Set up a summary record on a spreadsheet program. Consider using the following headings: CAR #; Description/Title; Date of original issue; Target date (plan for CA, test CA, deploy CA, verify effectiveness of CA); Person responsible, and Status & Date. Update the spreadsheet every month. Keep track of revised dates or number of times extended (for example: R2 after the date to show it is the second revision). Circulate the summary to management. Note: The test date is the date the solution was tested by trial, simulation, review, or other. The deploy date is when there was full scale implementation of the change. The verify date is when it was determined that the changes fixed the problem and that the action was effective.

Some type of reevaluation of the auditors' techniques is important through observing their performance during an audit or from the results of customer feedback and review of deliverables (reports). It should answer questions such as whether the best audit teams (experienced, knowledgable) were assembled for the best results in each audit and whether performance is consistent between audit teams.

Second Party.   The purpose of many second-party audits is to verify contractual relationships, assess capability of potential suppliers, compare different suppliers, and/or verify ongoing requirements. Supplier surveys are conducted to qualify new suppliers and are not rigorous quality system audits (nor should they be). For second-party audits, improvement of the auditee organization's process may not be one of the variables considered.

The performance of a supplier can be measured by the resulting quality (or cost of poor quality) of the materials and services supplied to customers. Supplier core (key suppliers') performance could be benchmarked against another organization's supplier core performance. Effectiveness of corrective actions taken from audits may be monitored to measure program effectiveness, as discussed for first-party audits. If you are building partnerships with your suppliers, you should move ahead to monitoring performance improvement of the supplier organization.

SIDEBAR

Organizations are conducting performance-based supplier audits. The idea is to move away from compliance audits to audits that are more directly related to the interest of the customer and supplier. In some cases the supplier agrees to a performance-based contract and is audited to the promises in the contract. Other performance-based audits are more analytical and assess organization objectives and their deployment. Some use the term management audit to denote the assessment of effectiveness. Still others have used the term value-added audits for both first and second party audits. The audit conventions for performance-based audits is not well defined.

Third Party. The purpose of most third-party audits is to independently verify compliance to a standard (ISO 9001, AS, TL, TE, DS, QS, quality award criteria), law, code, or regulation. Most third-party audit organizations readily admit that they are concerned with compliance—whether the designed process is adequate to meet the standard requirements and is implemented and maintained. Auditing the effectiveness (process capability and results) of a system against organizational goals is beyond the purpose of their audit. Once an outside organization (third party) goes beyond the written performance standard and its implementation and starts to compare performance to business goals and objectives, it is on shaky ground. Reports can become subjective and erroneous because outside audit organizations don't know your business.

Third-party audit organizations do need to monitor their own audit program customer satisfaction levels, because it is their business. Third-party audit organizations should monitor their program to ensure that customer requirements are met, customer expectations are addressed, and they provide maximum value (utility) audit service for their customers. Things to measure include the following:

- Fulfilling the contract terms
- Identifying customer expectations—many third-party organizations expanded their services to include QS-9000 and ISO 14000 audit services to address market/customer needs
- Maximizing value to the customer: being on time and not wasting customer time/resources, clear deliverables (reports), seeking other accreditations or mutual recognitions, competitive pricing, flexible schedule, using auditors with appropriate industry experience, increasing the knowledge and skills of auditors, and professionalism during audits

A tool that can be used by all audit organizations is a customer evaluation form (see Figure 7.3). You can use this example or design your own. The point is that there are certain things a good auditor will always do regardless of the audit outcome. Sure, a customer that is unhappy with the audit outcome may use the form to unfairly criticize the auditor, but this is not as likely as you may believe. And, sure, the auditors will feel some added pressure to do what they are supposed to do—but that's their job. The questions on the evaluation form should match with the auditor's duties (service provider) and the auditee's expectations (customer requirements). Additional evaluation question examples are in Appendix C. Management should use the evaluation form results to note trends and places where additional training and resources may be needed—data analysis that may lead to actions that prevent problem occurrence (preventive action).

You will need to audit the audit process—yes, assess the auditors. The evaluation should include the documented procedures (how the auditors are supposed to perform), the implementation of the process (what is actually being done), and individual auditor performance (to identify training needs). In short, identify problems and take corrective action. The audit of the audit function should be used as a management tool for improvement—sounds familiar, doesn't it? The audit function should be treated as an organization that provides a personal service to customers for a fee. The checklists in Appendices E through G can be used to audit the audit function.

For evaluating internal audit functions you can use trained auditors from other locations or auditors from neighboring organizations. The main challenge in assigning auditors to do the job is following the no-vested-interest rule. A simple solution is to use outside consultants that perform audits and have a good reputation.

AUDITING SURVEY FORM

Date of the Audit: _____ Area Audited: _____

1. Were you notified in advance that there was going to be an audit? (Yes/No)

2. Were you notified of the audit: purpose, scope, start and end times, (Yes/No)
   the performance standards used, team members?
   Comments?

3. Was an opening meeting held? (Yes/No)

4. Did the auditor keep you informed of major findings during the audit? (Yes/No)
   Comments?

5. Was there an exit meeting? (Yes/No)
   Comments?

6. Did the auditor(s) leave a draft of the audit results? (Yes/No)

7. Were you informed of when to expect the final report? (Yes/No)

8. Were the auditors courteous to interviewees? (Yes/No)

9. Would you be willing to be audited by the same team again? (Yes/No)
   Comments?

	Poor	Excellent
10. Were the stated audit objectives (purpose & scope) met?	1.....2.....3.....4.....5	
11. Did the auditor(s) act professionally at all times?	1.....2.....3.....4.....5	
12. As a service, how would you rate the audit?	1.....2.....3.....4.....5	

12. As a service, how would you rate the audit?
    Comments?

Please share your suggestions for improving the service.

Your Name: _____ Telephone Number: _____

Figure 7.3. Audit evaluation form.

The most important measure of the audit program is analyzing the overall program effectiveness to determine the following:

- Linkage of COR benefits to corrective actions implemented
- The degree to which planned corrective actions are effective the first time
- To what level the expected benefits were achieved
- If underlying cause(s) were addressed the first time
- The number of repeat problems due to the same cause
- The number of recycled corrective actions (didn't get it right the first time)
- Planned completion of corrective actions compared to actual completion—not the length of time corrective actions are open, because different problems will require different resolution times

Identification of actual cost reductions, opportunities and risks avoided (COR) provides an objective measure of the audit program's effectiveness. A program manager can demonstrate a savings to the company through the COR issues identified and resolved. These are meaningful measures of effectiveness that have much greater value than the number of audits conducted and numbers of nonconformances identified.

By analyzing the corrective action process from audits, you may identify negative trends that call for preventive action. Preventive actions would result in improvement of the overall improvement process (problem identification to resolution). If you don't analyze the program results, you will never know whether it is actually working. We have implied that the audit program function analyzes the results of corrective actions, but another department (or departments) could do the analysis as long as the audit program people receive the results.

If we can monitor corrective actions for effectiveness so that the same nonconformities do not happen again, we can also monitor the effectiveness of the audit program. The trap to avoid is measuring audit program effectiveness by the number of nonconformities reported or adherence to procedures.

Materials and Services

An audit is a personalized service and, as such, there are only a few incoming materials, such as paper, forms, report binders, sales brochures, toner cartridges, pens, clipboards, performance standards, and so on. If we expand the definition of materials to include incoming purchased services, then this area becomes more significant. Many audit organizations use an outside service organization to make travel arrangements. Implementation of controls concerning travel agencies may seem trivial until the customer wants to know why it is being charged for first-class tickets, the auditor was a day late because the agency limits its airline selection to those that give them big commissions, or you didn't know that rental car damage insurance was charged to your credit card and the travel agent automatically signed everyone up with full coverage just to be on the safe side. Another service that at first appears minor is repair and maintenance of the photocopy machine. Poorly maintained photocopy equipment can cause significant internal inefficiencies, and a poorly reproduced report can make a bad impression on customers.

Equipment (Machinery) and Technology

This is another part of the process that may appear to be less important to personal service organizations. However, as mentioned previously, the quality, reliability, and capability of reproduction equipment is critical to any service organization that issues reports or training materials as its product. Adding new technology such as two-sided reproductions and color copies is another way to serve customers.

If we look at other potential areas for improvement, you may want to switch from using a clipboard to a notebook computer. This can significantly reduce the cycle time from interview to report. Additionally, using a notebook computer with fax/modem capabilities opens the possibility for electronic communications and E-mail. Auditors who are traveling can pick up detailed messages each day and forward mail to the home office or to customers, which avoids "telephone tag" and completely resolves one-way communications. Using notebook computers brings us one step closer to real-time reporting. A detailed discussion of this topic is in chapter 8.

Environment

Here, think about the overall environment of quality auditing. To maximize audit program effectiveness, a positive, team-oriented environment should be established within the organization. Look at possible root causes for a negative environment and ensure that initiatives are in place to eliminate the causes. A negative environment will occur when individual auditors think their job is to identify rule breakers and determine the punishment. Training should address attitude issues so that auditors know that they are not only auditors but also emissaries of the audit department. Remember that if the audit program manager has an enforcer attitude it will prevail in the attitudes of the individual auditors.

Just as the audit program manager has expectations of the auditors, the auditors have expectations of audit program management. Auditors expect and should be provided with sufficient time to do a professional job in good working conditions. Ergonomics is another important factor for ensuring audit program effectiveness.

Consider setting up interdepartmental/function forums to exchange ideas, concerns, and suggestions regarding the quality of the audit process. The forum participants could be auditors, customers of the audit process, and suppliers to the auditors (management). Forums could be held several times each year, perhaps quarterly. The use of forums could fall under methods or measures, but we believe using them would have a significant effect on the participative environment created concerning the audit process. Forums can bring continuous improvement home to the audit function. (You would think that the organizations judging quality system adequacies would be totally immersed in continuous quality improvement, but for the majority this is often not the case.)

Audit Program Management Planning

An audit program plan incorporates the process activities and system activities and links them to organizational/functional objectives. A good start is to develop a mission statement for the quality audit function. We have talked about the audit program providing a service to customers (auditee, audit program boss, the organization, management), so put it in writing. The mission statement should align with the organization's objectives. Here is an example mission statement.

> The audit function will provide professional auditing services that continuously meet customer requirements and assure conformance to company and external standards.

Implicit in this statement is the need to define the audit program customers and document their requirements (expectations). Additionally, the statement indicates that meeting requirements is ongoing and continuous. To achieve your mission, you will need to establish objectives and a plan for achieving the objectives.

For example: The following objectives and strategies may be established to meet customer requirements (auditees, client, management), and continually improve and assure conformance.

Objective A: Improve the relevancy of audits to the auditing customers.

Strategy 1: Develop feedback systems (auditee, client, management)

Strategy 2: Upgrade auditor skills for observing and reporting performance issues

Strategy 3: Link audit scheduling and reporting to customer interests

Objective B: Improve the effectiveness of the auditing function

Strategy 1: Establish goals for audit program and report progress

Strategy 2: Re-engineer auditing process to identify bottlenecks and redundancy

Strategy 3: Identify new value-added auditing services

Objective C: Maintain continuous compliance with fewer resources

Strategy 1: Participate in new projects to identify compliance needs

Strategy 2: Monitor continuous compliance to identify areas for reduced auditing

Strategy 3: Utilize non internal auditing inputs to attest to compliance levels

Management's job is to steer the ship. Unfortunately, people are not always as responsive as the rudder of a ship. Management must utilize the six system actuators to accomplish its objectives. The system actuators are:

1. Provide direction (rules, directives, methods, and so on)—not too many, not too few, not too restrictive, not too prescriptive; just enough that people don't flounder.

2. Plan future activities (organizational changes, future initiatives)—plan, plan, and then plan again. The first part of the PDCA cycle molds the future. Planning can include business/department plans, quality plans, operational plans, and strategic plans. Plans define future activities and goals.

3. Train people (web based training, classroom, video, banners, messages, pep talks)—identify training needs beyond the individual processes to ensure that people get a message consistent with organizational goals and which meets societal needs.

4. Provide resources (people, organizational structure, equipment, technology, fixed assets, monetary wealth). Managing resources is a major responsibility of the system and can have a significant effect on the success of the individual processes. No matter how capable a process, if the wealth of the organization is mismanaged you are still bankrupt.

5 Set up incentive systems (reward, recognition and punishment)—every organization has incentive systems; some

are good and some are bad. Compensation levels and feelings about compensation affect the type of people you retain and attract. Most organizations cannot afford to pay the highest or the lowest compensation.

6. Provide feedback (performance measures, audits, financial, output results). Feedback is used in many forms to constantly fine-tune outputs to achieve the optimal desired results.

Rarely can you rely on one method to achieve the desired behavior. Therefore, the quality audit program plan should incorporate a number of approaches to achieve the desired results (meeting established objectives). No matter how capable the individual process, a capable system must be in place to make things work.

When you are ready, the quality program plan should address integrating of continuous quality improvement with the audit process. Excerpted from *The Quality Master Plan,* integration steps include the following:[22]

- Communicate the mission of the audit function to everyone.
- Ensure that established policies and guidelines are consistent with quality principles.
- Foster a continuous improvement style of management versus a once-and-done mentality.
- Seek to limit short-term thinking and remedial corrective actions regarding internal and external customer issues.
- Establish teams where appropriate (when the organization benefits from it) for achieving improved service performance.
- Support teams by providing training and resources to accomplish quality objectives.
- Incorporate quality management objectives into marketing, sales (third party), and service performance strategies.
- Include quality objectives in job descriptions and individual performance requirements.
- Structure the organization for improved customer responsiveness (by customers, by markets, and so on).

Organizing Work Flow

The organizational structure should be customer and market focused. Many service organizations are infamous for the bureaucracy they put their customers through (internal focus versus external customer focus).

There has been improvement in the service sector, but it is slow. Recent bad examples include the following.

- The collection agency. In one case a customer received a call from the supplier of a postage machine. The customer was informed that its account was 90 days past due and was asked what would be done about it. The customer checked its accounting records and found that payment was made and that the postage machine supplier had cashed the check. The response from the other end of the telephone was that the payment amount was not correct and it went into a special account. Again, "When are you going to pay the 90-days-overdue invoice?" "But you were paid, even if it was for $1.63 more than the invoice called for." The person said that wasn't her department and that she expected the overdue bill to be resolved or else.

- Bad news auditor. The registrar's auditor showed up two hours late and didn't call ahead. The auditor refused to come in at 7:30 A.M. (originally scheduled for 8:00) to meet with senior managers and told the customer contact that she didn't start till 9:00 A.M. anyway. The next day, she trashed a test and calibration procedure and told the auditee that it was all wrong (it had been approved by other qualified registrars). To top it off, she argued with her boss on the conference room telephone as everyone listened.

- Absentee answering. Answering machines are driving me batty. One day I used a cellular phone to call six people. None of them answered the telephone. I was automatically transferred to an answering machine or to an electronic mailbox, without forewarning, which means I must redial my credit card number for each new call instead of being able to hit the pound key. Another thing that bugs me are answering systems that walk you through multiple levels of menu choices. Once I get to my choice, I am in no mood to wait another five minutes until someone answers.

The point is that the audit function provides a service. You should define and then check all the customer interfaces to ensure that customer requirements and expectations are met: inquiry, confirming requirements, resolving problems, performing the service, providing deliverables (the report), invoicing (or intercompany transfers), and collecting.

High-Performance Teams/Natural Work Groups

The new team concepts for the workplace are taking hold. Organizations are claiming many advantages to forming teams and giving people more say in how activities are performed. To implement these programs, people are being trained in topics like total quality management, quality awareness, team building, organizational mission and objectives, customer satisfaction, continuous improvement, and empowerment, to name a few. If we invest in giving people the skills, knowledge, and latitude to do their job, improvement will result. Some organizations claim a 30-to-1 payback for every training dollar. The idea is to move more decisions down to where they should be made.

Some programs that are intended to develop high-performance teams are misdirected, with the goal to eliminate the supervisor position. These are usually called self-directed teams. The fundamental flaw is that someone—supervisor, coach, section leader—has to provide direction to the teams. We cannot eliminate this interface, no matter how painful the interface. The interface person between management and the workers doesn't have a glamorous position and is normally the bearer of bad news. The person who provides the interface needs to give directions that not all the workers will like and has to report problems and issues to managers that they will not like. There will always need to be interaction between the team sponsor and the team leader for continued improvement and higher levels of performance. Organizations need to continue with team training plus provide training to managers, supervisors, section leaders, and team leaders. Those that devote time to help make leaders better leaders will win, both within the organization and in the marketplace.

The audit program management may want to consider natural work teams. No matter how the teams are structured—by region (area), market segment (customer, product), or type of service (preassessment, compliance, standard)—an increase in performance can be expected.

Organizational Changes

Due to the requirement of independence, the code of ethic requirements to remain unbiased and the need to ensure effectiveness of the audit program, personnel changes are a necessary ingredient in audit program planning. Many third-party audit organizations rotate auditors among clients to ensure that subsequent audits are professional and unbiased. We applaud them for this initiative. This prevents loss of objectivity from developing that will detract from the power of the independent audits.

This is a consideration for first- and second-party audits, too. Auditors need to be rotated and replaced to ensure professionally unbiased observations.

A second factor affecting personnel changes is auditor burnout. Management should be looking for signs of burnout after about two years. Compliance auditors should be given different responsibilities after about four years to give them other experiences and to keep them from getting into a rut. We have seen too many cases where career auditors get so set in their ways that they reject all new ideas for improvement.

Reporting: The Big Picture

Everything we have discussed so far (defining process elements, audit program planning) all comes together when you give your annual report to management. Management wants to know the following:

- What did you do for me last year? How did the department contribute to the organization?
- Is there anything management needs to know to avoid risks to the organization's wealth (new regulations, defunct programs)?
- What will you do for the organization next year? How will you contribute?

If you have identified measures that relate to organizational objectives, this information will be easy to assemble. Management wants to know how the audit program is contributing to the ROI (return on investment). Management is not interested in how many audits are going to be performed next year or that you plan a 20 percent increase in the number of findings.

Summary

In summary, we can ensure audit program effectiveness if we do the following:

- Track the open corrective/preventive actions.
- Define audit program goals and objectives.
- Identify and control key performance parameters.
- Standardize methods.

- Identify measures and ensure that they relate to organizational goals and customer needs.
- Get feedback from customers (client, management, auditee).
- Compare audit program results with objectives.
- Report performance to management regularly.
- Assume responsibility for success and be accountable for performance.

We have provided a checklist for auditing your audit program and auditor qualifications in Appendix F and G. Appendix F is a checklist from ISO 10011-2 (assessor qualification guidelines), and Appendix G is taken from ISO 10011-3[23] (assessment program guidelines).

Chapter 8

Closing the Loop on the Audit Process

It may seem that we have exhausted every possible reason for ineffective corrective actions from audits, but that is not the case. Practicing what we preach, we built a cause-and-effect diagram to identify all potential causes of ineffective corrective action from audits. First, we stated the problem (or defect):

> Problem statement: Ineffective corrective action from investigations has resulted in the waste of organizational resources and organizations are not benefitting from the management audit process.

We then constructed a cause-and-effect diagram and listed the major causes for an ineffective corrective action process. The causes were grouped under methods, measures, people, machines, materials, and environment. In prior chapters we have discussed all of the major causes of the problem except the following:

- Auditors are resistant to changing from the noncompliance list to identification of systemic problems. (This was placed in the people category although it could also be an environmental or business culture issue.)
- Management does not give audits and close-out a priority.

- Audit organizations are not using the latest technology. (Not using modern communication technology does not mean the corrective action process will fail, but use of the technology will enhance effectiveness.)
- The work environment is not conducive to improving operations.
- Results of investigations are used to penalize stakeholders.

Refer to the cause-and-effect diagram, Figure 8.1, to note the highlighted causes to be discussed in this chapter.

Compliance Auditing

External compliance audits may be conducted by government agencies, customers or independent third-party audit organizations (certification or registration). The face-to-face audits give us added confidence that organizations are in compliance with the regulation, contract, agreement, or standard.

Internal compliance audits are conducted by organizations to help them prepare for the external audits. The internal compliance audits assess the degree of compliance to external standards. Degree of compliance is determined by the adequacy of the defined system, its implementation, and on-going maintenance. The idea is for the organization to emulate the external compliance audits to better prepare people for the external auditors. Many judge the success of an internal compliance audit program by the number of noncompliances issued by the external audit organizations. The goal is to achieve continuous compliance to the external standard(s). In this way the internal compliance program and external conformity assessment process are working together for a common goal. However, the process becomes adversarial as soon as the external auditing organization detects a noncompliance.

None of the comments in this book should be taken to mean that we do not support compliance auditing or the conformity assessment process. Our point in this book is that you cannot make compliance auditing into something it is not. The focus is on compliance to an external standard and not effectiveness of internal organizational processes. The adversarial nature of external compliance auditing prevents it from ever becoming a team approach for improvement.

The proposed 2000 draft international standard for ISO 9001 spells out the same minimum requirements we have discussed in this section.

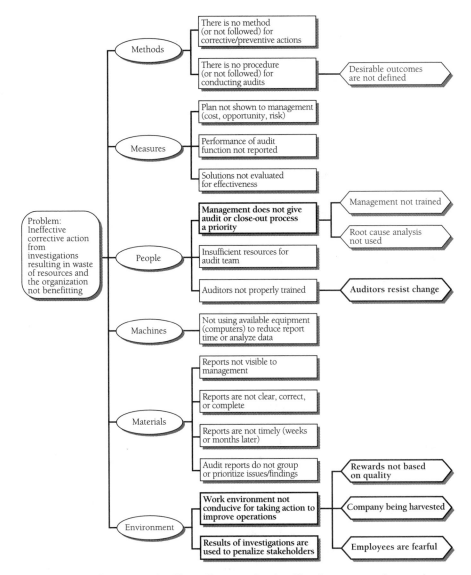

Figure 8.1. Cause-and-effect diagram for ineffective corrective action.

Organizations are required to conduct internal audits to ensure the (quality management) system, as implemented and maintained, conforms to the requirements of the international standard. However, the standard does not limit your internal audit program (or any organization initiative) to the minimum requirements in the international ISO 9001 standard.

Auditors Making Compliance Audits Better

Auditors and audit program organizations can make compliance audits better by following proper audit conventions as spelled in ISO 19011 (ISO 10011) and conforming to a code of ethics. We have also noticed that the nature of the compliance audit process can be the auditor's undoing. This natural characteristic (present in most compliance audits) of a compliance audit can result in very annoying if not unprofessional behavior on the part of the compliance auditor without their knowledge. This characteristic is the auditee's accommodating and attentive behavior toward the auditor. Many auditors interpret this solicitous behavior as common courtesy, but it goes far beyond that. Auditors should be watchful for developing negative personality traits that detract from effectiveness of the audit. When audit program managers observe the following behavior in auditors, they should point out areas for self-improvement to the auditor.

Feelings of self-importance: Because of the attention and courtesy shown the compliance auditor, it is easy for the auditor to feel a sense of self-importance. Auditees listen to every word spoken by the auditor to both indulge the auditor and to prepare for any disagreements. It feels good to be treated as an all-knowing revered expert. Auditors must remember that the relationship is artificial due to the lack of equity in the business relationship.

Know-it-all behavior: Auditors should not share their views on life, quality improvement, crime, automobiles, race cars, diet plans, or any topic not related to the audit. It is easy to be a know-it-all because the auditee will yield to the desire and opinions of the auditor. In a compliance audit environment, the auditee is not going to risk disagreeing with the opinions (not audit related) expressed by the auditor.

Boasting: We have observed compliance auditors boast of their accomplishments to the auditee (present company included). If there are no issues regarding the compliance auditor's qualifications, no boasting is necessary. Boasting may include comment such as: I have computed over 500 audits, I am on all the ISO committees, I know important people, etc.

Given the nature of the work and the lack of equity between the auditee and auditor, it is easy to see how some auditors could become egotistical and self-righteous. All auditors and regulators should be on guard for the above behaviors.

Overcoming Redundent Audits

Some audit programs lose their zip and become monotonous. It is a result of our propensity to form a comfort zone and a way of doing things to reduce stress and build confidence.

All too frequently audits can become the same old thing audit after audit: looking at the same area, asking the same questions, talking to the same people, and getting the same answers. It is like selecting a path on the map to go from one place to another and never changing. The first time you take the path it is pretty interesting and you can learn a lot. The second time less so, and after a while everything looks the same except for the occasional road work or new building going up. It is the same with auditing. If the audit method is always the same for the same function, nothing new will be learned. The key to effective ongoing audits is mixing up the path.

Mixing up the path can be taking a different route, even if it is longer: Perhaps a more scenic route; going backwards or starting from the middle; or selecting different auditors or different standards to audit against. Try different perspectives: Fly instead of drive; View the overall picture instead of examining things with a microscope; or check out the new road that was just completed (such as a new product, new service, or new process).

For audits to be effective we need to form habits that require change. Following the same audit path every time will reduce effectiveness, while changing paths will improve it.

Transition from Compliance Audits

On two different occasions, clients have told us that they were instructed by trainers of audit classes to hide the bad stuff in the ladies' rest room when the third-party auditor came to town. This is not only sexist (assumes the auditor is male), but it strikes at the very core of why compliance audits have limited effect on the actual performance of an organization. There is absolutely no added value in hiding boxes of records. In fact, it is a drain on resources because you must remember to hide the records every time the auditor shows up.

This mind-set, and everything that emanates from it, is a particular problem for regulated organizations. They have been taught to do what the auditors say, not to think for themselves, and to hide stuff if necessary to stay off the auditor's "hit list" (get a citation). Compliance audits are not going to be eliminated because it is a necessary control to ensure the public's well being or to ensure contractual terms are being met between two organizations. However, the scope of compliance audits must be limited to specified requirements and not the individual auditor's interpretation.

The reason for differentiating between compliance audits and management-performance type audits is to be able to communicate the differences to the customers of the audit (auditee). Being able to shift the auditee's mind-set between compliance and management audits is just as important as the attitude of the auditors. No matter how good the auditor's intentions are while doing a management audit, the auditor will have limited success if all the auditee answers are pat, and guarded answers are provided that would appease regulators.

Compliance auditing has increased societal confidence that certain products (food, drugs, etc.) and services (medical) are safe. However, any increase in performance has been small compared to the high cost of compliance auditing programs. Improved performance and cost-effective reliability will only come from management-performance audits. Management system audits can double and triple performance, whereas compliance audits seek to maintain the status quo or may even result in the lessening of performance by adding unnecessary requirements.

If you want to start using management-performance audits, here are some tips.

1. Train auditors how to conduct quality management system audits. Unfortunately, some career compliance auditors will not accept the new ideas introduced in the training and should either remain as compliance auditors or be replaced. For private industry, the acceptance level may be as high as 75 percent, but for compliance inspectors the acceptance level of this new approach will be much lower. We are not saying that compliance auditors are neither intelligent nor sincere, it is just that they have been doing auditing a certain way for a number of years. The methods have worked for them, and it is difficult to change.

2. Inform management of the difference between compliance audits and management audits. Tell them how you expect the organization to benefit. Tell managers that management audits will focus on the system and that it is important that no one be

singled out for punishment. This last part is important because management has normally reacted to a noncompliance and sought the guilty party.

3.   Differentiate between compliance audits and management audits. The message to the auditee must be that it is important to share information to uncover system problems that in turn can be fixed. It is also important that auditees know they will not be punished and that there will be no accusations or finger-pointing.

4.   Unfortunately, you may need to secure your internal management audit results from regulators because they will use them against you. By secure, we mean that the distribution of your audit reports will need to be controlled. Audit reports should be marked confidential and you may want to put them in binders that have closures so that any regulator discovering an internal audit report would have to physically open the binder. The existence of audit reports can be a legal liability in a court of law. Once the corrective action is completed (the audit is closed out) the audit report should be archived in a confidential storage area unless legal counsel recommends its destruction (shredding). Corrective action records are lower risk since they only record improvements to the process or system.

5.   To help bring about government agencies' understanding of the benefits of management quality system audits, you will need to move slowly but deliberately. To start with, a plan will need to be developed to overcome existing adversarial relationships between the regulating organization and subcontractor. Next, you will need to separate the inspectors (compliance auditors) from the quality management system auditors. It would be inappropriate for someone to conduct a quality system audit one month, then go back to the same subcontractor the next month and conduct a compliance audit (it won't work). The benefits of quality system audits will be more reliable products and lower cost. The mission of the compliance program should be redefined to focus only on specified requirements and to give subcontractors more latitude to appeal noncompliances if the intent of the requirement is being met. Compliance audits should have a well-defined purpose and scope in order to maximize their benefit and minimize their damage.

We know of government agencies that have redefined their mission to include both compliance and improvement for the public good. They have maintained their compliance program, but added programs for helping and improving performance of supplier organizations. Some programs help newly regulated companies, others help with the release of new products, and some focus on performance auditing.

6. On the flip side of the coin, subcontractors have resisted making changes by claiming any change will cost more and, therefore, the government will need to pay more. This is a defense tactic to ward off abuses by inspectors, but it is used all too frequently, even when the subcontractor knows it will benefit the organization in the long run.

This is not the place to debate the benefits of continuous quality improvement principles compared to inspecting quality into products. It is a fact that a process under statistical control can provide a more reliable and consistent product at a lower cost than a process that relies on inspection after the fact to achieve quality. Yet, regulated industries rely almost totally on inspection. Many don't understand continuous quality improvement and will argue the merits of inspecting everything. It is in the best interest of taxpayers that this debate take place to put inspection in its place so that the general public can benefit from more reliable products at a lower cost.

What If Quality Audits Are Not a Priority to Management?

It is up to you to sell management on the merits of management quality audits (performance audits). While reading this book is a good start, it should be followed-up with training of upper and middle managers. Training is important so that management can better manage the audit process and so that they know what is expected of them. We know of companies that put their entire management group through a two-day internal audit class, while others can't be bothered. If your management is in the latter category, do what most of them do to get a new idea accepted: get permission to start a pilot program. Then, based on the success of the pilot program, you can expand it to other operations.

One auditor shared with us a technique for increasing the likelihood that there would be corrective action of the audit findings. In this case, the auditor requires that management identify the resources that will address the findings from the proposed audit before the audit takes place. If there is no commitment of resources, then there is no audit. Also, the people assigned to the corrective action team must be some of the best people in the organization. Then, the lead auditor conducts a workshop with senior management to explain the audit process, follow-up actions, the potential benefits, and what to expect. Finally, management is required to set the objectives of the audit. Then, and only then, is the audit conducted. Not all of us have the flexibility to refuse to conduct an audit, but these are some good ideas that you may want to explore.

Staying Current with the Latest Technology

With the popularity and affordability of computers, there has been an explosion of new communication tools available to auditors. We do not purchase every new gimmick, but we are constantly looking for value-added technology that will make quality audits more effective and efficient. Specifically, look for technology that will reduce audit cycle time, reduce paper, and improve the effectiveness of the audit. Here are a few.

Communication Technology

Electronic Mail. E-mail allows auditors to communicate with all the people involved in an audit prior to and after the audit. It is excellent for one-way communication and is a move toward real-time reporting (being more responsive) of deliverables. A person can send and receive messages from anyone around the globe. Using e-mail requires the user to check their mailbox periodically (at least ever other day). You can use e-mail anytime, so you are not limited to business hours.

E-mail is also very useful for sending deliverables (audit plans, audit reports) to the auditee in a timely manner. It is a great time saver. If you get a message you can send a reply instantly (no need to write down "Call Jan" on your to-do list), and a report can be sent via e-mail or via fax/modem without printing, stuffing, stamping, and mailing.

It is also possible to attach files to the message. If the receiver of the message with an attached file has the same software or is able to convert your software, they will be able to read your report or letter in the original format. You can attach anything from an entire book to presentation slides. When the receiver gets the message, they can read the attached file with their own software. It is quick, easy (most of the time) and extremely useful when time and cost is a factor. While writing this book, we were able to exchange chapters by attaching files to messages in a matter of minutes for less than a dollar.

E-mail capability and internet providers allow you to participate in discussion groups and to access web sites. Discussion lists can keep you up-to-date on what is going on in the audit world. You can access ASQ's and other organization's home page and be able to download or read on line a wealth of information.

Fax/Modem. Using a fax/modem makes for prettier reports and letters because it will fax whatever is on your computer directly to a fax machine. You do not need to worry about converting a file to ASCII in order to send a letter or report. You can send a fax to one person or, by using address books, send a fax to an entire group of people. You can send your audit plan, audit report, and checklist instantly from your computer and they will arrive just like you formatted them, which is a necessity if you want your deliverables to look their best.

Voice Mail. Voice mail, like e-mail, allows remote retrieval of messages but it is limited to one-way voice communications. Some people prefer being able to call a voice mailbox and listen to messages. Certainly, by listening to another person's voice, you may be able to detect the need to respond or the urgency of a certain matter better than you would with e-mail. However, some people are wordy on voice mail and take up a lot of space (time), which is less likely to happen with e-mail.

Cellular Telephones. Cellular telephone technology allows a person to take or receive calls from almost anywhere. Cellular telephones are useful in situations when an auditor needs to be able to contact the client or audit coordinator quickly. They are also useful when the auditor is auditing a large or remote facility where telephones are not easily accessible. Cellular telephones can increase productivity for persons who experience a lot of waiting time (airline, office, vehicle).

Audit Software

Audit software is starting to pop up everywhere, but we have yet to find a program that we like. You should view audit software as you would working papers. Working papers need to be flexible and should not, in any way, detract from the effectiveness of the audit. Every software package evaluated to-date has severe limitations. The last one J. P. evaluated: (1) had a canned checklist that could not be changed or bypassed; (2) had a scoring system that could not be bypassed (not even for one question); and (3) the reports were lousy and it was very difficult to export the report to another software (to fix the format). In short, the use of the software would have made the audit report less effective. Our advice is to keep looking until someone listens to the customer (auditors).

Digital Cameras

You can now purchase a digital camera to connect to a notebook computer. You can take pictures with the camera and then see the picture (color, if you have it) materialize on your computer screen. This is not a toy and will become a serious tool for auditors. With this device you can take pictures of problems (the rusty container, defect, damage, etc.) while you are auditing. In turn, the pictures can be shown at the exit meeting and/or included in your report. This power to bring the problem to management is yet in its infancy stages. This device should do a lot to improve the effectiveness of quality audits.

From Clipboard to Computer: A Discussion on the Use of Computers

Just as the slide rule and, later, the calculator changed the way we do things, so have computers. Computers are another tool in the evolution of the communication age. Portable computers are now the size of some textbooks and hand held (palm) computers are the size of calculators.

Using modern auditing equipment such as the personal computer (PC) and its related equipment (for example, software, electronic mail systems, printers, etc.) can improve the efficiency and effectiveness of the audit process. The use of the computer can save audit time in the preparation and reporting phases. Some computer programs read hand writing for those that have not mastered the keyboard yet. The computer also allows for customizing the auditor's checklist making the audit more meaningful.

Computers are becoming affordable for everyday use with the right size and power to be an effective tool for improving quality system audits. Auditors must use PCs if they are to remain competitive. Just as companies must continuously improve, so must the auditing process.

1. Preparation before the audit. First, you will need the proper equipment and know how to use it.

     Hardware (suggested)

> Computer (notebook or handheld) MB RAM, mouse)
> Portable printer (such as a bubble jet or laser)
> Fax/modem card or other electronic interface with
> connectors
>
> Software (suggested)
> Word processing software (99 percent of audit work)
> Spreadsheet software (analyzing data)
> Forms generator software (corrective action forms, etc.)
> Flowchart software (analyze procedures)
>
> Other items you will need include
> Floppy disks
> Paper
> Clipboard or notepad

If you are not already familiar with how to use this equipment, some training will be needed. You will need to understand the operating system and the software that you have selected. Once you have mastered their use, you will find that computers can be used in all types of audits (first-, second-, and third-party, internal and external).

Next, as with any audit, you will determine the purpose of the audit, the scope of the audit, identify the performance standards, and assemble the audit team. You can start by using the equipment during the development of your checklist and putting together the audit plan and notification letter (deliverables prior to the audit). The audit plan and notification letter can be put on the computer software and sent to the auditee by e-mail, fax/modem, or post carrier (such as U.S. Mail or express mail). If the auditee wants to make some changes to the audit plan, you can make the changes to the computer file while you are talking to the auditee on the telephone, then transmit the new version electronically at the end of the conversation (no hand-written changes that must be given to a secretary to type and reissue). In your notification letter, you should request a conference room or office for the auditor(s) that has a table, a telephone with the capability to connect to a modem, and electrical outlets for operating the PC.

Putting checklist questions on word processing software or spreadsheet software allows you to tailor the checklist questions for each audit. You can create a library of checklist questions for specific elements of various performance standards and not "reinvent the wheel" for each audit. Prior to interviewing the auditee, review the quality system documents. Add questions directly related to the auditee's quality system. This helps you create a customized checklist for each audit that will be more professional and more effective. Furthermore, if a procedure is not clear (difficult to understand), you can use your computer software to flowchart the process. Flowcharting will help you understand the process steps and identify system weaknesses in the procedures that are evaluated prior to the on-site interview.

At some point prior to the audit, a detailed audit schedule should be issued, showing who will be interviewed when and where or what work operation will be observed. The detailed schedule can be put on the word processing software or a spreadsheet. These can be readily updated on-the-spot when necessary.

Other documents such as auditor qualifications and auditor recertification records can be input and stored on personal computers. Then, resumés and auditor records can be updated as needed. Providing up-to-date auditor credentials (resumé and records) adds another degree of professionalism.

When there is an audit team of two or more people, the other team members can also be outfitted with the proper equipment and trained in its use. All audit team members should be provided with a disk which contains the setup for a common document format. It is important that everyone is working with the same information to save time when putting together the final report. However, it is only necessary that at least one auditor (preferably the lead auditor) be computer literate since the PC will not be used during the interview process.

Over time, you will develop standard templates and examples for the audit plan, checklist, and detailed schedule. These should be included in the quality audit program documents and should be controlled.

In summary, the computer can be used in the audit preparation stage to:

- Customize and update checklists to improve audit effectiveness.
- Better understand the process/procedures and analyze systems by using flowcharts.
- Issue the audit documents electronically to speed up communications and eliminate paper and postage.
- Keep documents and records current, such as the detailed audit schedule.
- Communicate through e-mail with the audit team and auditee to improve the coordination of the audit.

2. Start the Audit. It is advisable to arrive early at the auditee facility with your equipment and hard copies of the audit plan,

checklist, and detailed schedule. At this time, you can set up your equipment, make any changes to the detailed audit schedule (there usually are some), and print a new detailed schedule to be photocopied and handed out at the opening meeting. Some auditors leave the computer equipment in the office or hotel room and only use it to input the daily results of the interviews and evaluation of records. In our experience this is a mistake, as some change to the audit schedule is always required because someone is either visiting a customer, sick, or has been called away to attend a meeting unexpectedly.

The next step, of course, is to conduct the opening meeting. After the opening meeting, you can make any additional changes to the detailed schedule on the computer, print it, and ask the coordinator to distribute the new schedule to the interviewees.

3. Performing the Audit. The actual performance of the audit is conducted just as in the past. At this point, it is more effective to take the clipboard and checklist and leave the computer in the office. The computer is a machine and it intimidates interviewees. It would be great to take notes on the computer while you are asking questions, but it takes away from direct eye contact, makes you less mobile, and is too much like working as a court stenographer.

The computer can be used during team meetings to start writing up nonconformities or findings. Notes should be transferred to the computer as soon as possible to lessen the possibility of memory loss omissions and to improve effectiveness of the final report. These entries should be made in an organized manner for ease of locating and cross referencing by the audit team.

One audit organization conducts daily team meetings, usually in a hotel room after dinner until 11:00 p.m., during which the auditors present their nonconformities. Each nonconformity is discussed and reviewed and, when agreed upon, is entered into the computer so that a current record is maintained. The audit team results are printed and then discussed with the auditee organization the next day at a daily briefing.

4. Preparing for the Exit Meeting. In preparing for the exit meeting, it is critical to have all appropriate data in as complete, organized, and professional format as possible. One technique is

to gather the audited information from the audit team via a floppy disk with their results. You should allow at least two hours prior to the closing meeting to prepare the report. Part of that time is used to meet with the audit team members to add any additional nonconformities. When you do this for the first time, you may need additional time until you become proficient. The on-site time to prepare a report is offset by not needing four to eight hours (or even several weeks) after the audit to prepare a report at the home office.

Refer to the audit organization standard operating procedure or chapter 1 (Formatting and Organizing Reports) to determine what should be included in the audit report.

The introduction and background information normally included in an audit report should be prepared in advance. You should take the time to read through the report once and run a spell check. You will not have a finished, polished report ready for the exit meeting, but you will have a draft report that is nearly complete. Mark each page of the report with the word draft. However, you do not want to issue a draft report that is a rough draft (with typographical errors and incoherent sentences). If you need more time to compile the report, reschedule the exit meeting. Distributing a garbage report will have a negative impact instead of a positive one.

If you are ever going to experience printer problems, this is the time it normally occurs—right before the exit meeting. The most embarrassing moments occur when the lead auditor promised a report and no report can be provided because of printer problems. Contingency plans to overcome printer problems can include: (1) bringing along a back-up printer, (2) faxing the results to the auditee's fax machine, and/or (3) using the auditee's computer/printer equipment. The option that is least likely to succeed is being dependent on the use of the auditee's equipment.

5. The Audit Report. If you did everything else right, issuing the final report is a simple matter of editing the report to ensure that it is clear and correct. You should be able to send the final report the next morning.

In b.c. (before computers), auditors would return to the office with a set of notes. The auditor would decipher the notes, double-check with the audit team members about the meaning of the notes, write the report, send it to typing, wait, review for errors and correct them, send it back to typing, wait, review it again, sign it, and finally mail the audit report to the auditee. The time and cost differences between the old methods and computerized methods are self-evident.

Some audit organizations use check sheets to tally audit scores. Spreadsheet programs and some software can format the check sheets and add the audit scores automatically. This not only saves time, but also ensures consistency and accuracy of the results.

6. Follow-Up and Close-Out. The lead auditor should receive the corrective action plan for the findings. The corrective actions can be tracked using spreadsheet or database software.

7. Computerized Audit Program Management. It is critical that information be backed up on a daily basis. You cannot trust the hard drive, as it will crash at some point in time or your equipment may get damaged in transit.

Use e-mail and networking to coordinate audits and transmit information and reports (audit plan, final report, etc.). E-mail and networking speed up communication as we approach real time communication. Some audit organizations have put together tool boxes to help auditors with hotel interface problems when they want to upload or download information. The tool boxes consist of: (1) multiple outlet electrical adapter (hotel electrical outlets are scarce), (2) extension cord, (3) alligator clips to clip onto the tip-and-ring wires (or other clip-type device) if phone jacks have not been installed, (4) two screwdrivers (flat head and Phillips), and (5) extra telephone line cord. Telephone connector kits are available at local electronic stores.

The audit organization or the individual auditor should keep records of audits for recertification or for reaccreditation. This task can also be centralized and put on a communication network.

8. Tip Summary:

• Do not wait until the end of the week to start putting your data on the computer. Put it on the computer while it is fresh in your mind, then if you have questions, you can resolve them the next day.

- Back up your information on floppy disk and hard copy.
- Take a backup computer and printer or ensure that you have a contingency plan for equipment failures.
- Take extra application software disks in case the hard drive crashes.
- Avoid airport x-ray machines. Computer chips can be damaged, so you may want to let security personnel check the computer.
- Select a popular word processing software and stick with it. Talk to colleagues to find out what software is supported within your organization.
- The lead auditor needs to know computers.
- Any notebook computer should work, but customer satisfaction with computers is dropping because of some cheap models on the market. Stick with reliable computers from manufacturers with a good reputation.

What If the Environment for Quality Audits Is Not Right?

This is somewhat akin to the problem of management not giving follow-up audits a priority, but it could be much more serious. The environment could be wrong either because of upper management, market factors, or a workforce highly resistant to change.

Harvesting

If the organization is being harvested, there is nothing you can do about it. Harvesting is when management has decided that there is no future in the business. This could be because the product or service is obsolete, the market is disappearing, or the technology is obsolete and will be over-taken by organizations that have competitive technology. It is just a matter of time before the business closes down. If the business is making a modest profit, management may decide to keep the business operating until the market disappears or the company is driven out of the market for cost reasons. In this case, management will only keep the minimum resources in order to maximize profit in the final years of the business. Even in this case, management is still interested in improvement that has an immediate payback, but forget the long-term stuff (it doesn't meet the organizational objectives).

Rewards Based Only on ROE and Output

There is nothing wrong with having return on equity and output (volume) goals. But if these are the only goals, all decisions will be based on short-term payback. To maximize output goals in any given year, everything is sacrificed to get out the last pound, unit of product, or service. If ROE is the only goal, there is never a good reason to invest in the future since every penny spent on capital lowers the return on equity. Every organization needs to balance short-term needs with long-term needs.

Employees Are Fearful

Some managers still use the stick to motivate employees: "If you don't do what I want, you can be replaced." In such an environment, employees are afraid to make any decisions that the boss will not like. This type of culture will make it very difficult to put together an effective corrective action process. If people make the wrong suggestions, they could be labeled as troublemakers. There is not much you can do as an individual in this situation unless you are the boss. You should target the advantages of diverse options for building a stronger organization.

Reactive Management (Reacting to Findings)

This is a very common problem in organizations. Some managers moved up the ranks by creating a crisis and then solving that same crisis. The solution was to point the finger at someone else. If people are worried about protecting their back, they will not want to be audited because they know that if you uncover any findings they will be raked over the coals. This could be called the "hear no evil, see no evil, then no evil exists to speak of" organization. Many managers in these organizations do not want to know about problems because it implies that they manage imperfectly. Fortunately, not everyone is wearing rose-colored glasses. Management training must overcome these reactionary tactics of insecure managers. Managers that react to audit findings and try to lay blame will sabotage your efforts. Managers and supervisors who are under the gun will hide problems.

Summary

Compliance Audits

Compliance audits have a place in the audit world but should not be confused with management-performance type audits. Compliance auditing should not stop organizations from expanding to the benefits of management audits. The two types of audits should not be blended together because it will make a mess of both types of audits. Instead, their differences should be dealt with and managed.

Make Auditing a Priority

If management does not make quality auditing a priority, recognize that fact and make it your personal challenge to communicate the benefits of quality audits to management.

Audit Technology

Quality auditing is a service that requires a considerable amount of communication, so you should be interested in the latest technology. Consider using the following:

- Electronic mail
- Fax/modem
- Voice mail
- Audit software
- Digital cameras
- Notebook computers

Notebook Computers

Notebook computers can be a fantastic tool, but they have their challenges. First you need to learn how to use them. Then, resist the urge to constantly upgrade your hardware and software. Above all, keep data backed up.

If the Organizational Culture Is Not Right

There are situations in which quality audits will not work effectively, so there is no reason to keep banging your head against the wall.

Chapter 9

Epilogue: Back to the Future

Many organizations are spending an extreme amount of time fixing things we commonly refer to as "problems." These events may be nonconformities in the system which are concerns for us or our customers, but they keep us continually looking back, locked in the past. Whenever we experience problems, we are caught in the "past trap." We spend too much of our time trying to resolve issues that should have been addressed and resolved in the planning stage of our process, product, or service cycle. We have dedicated so many of our resources to addressing such issues that we hardly have time to address the concerns of today, let alone plan adequately for the future. If we examined the distribution of our time devoted to past, present and future activities, we would find the percentages to be as follows:

Time	Past	Present	Future
Activity	Corrective Actions, Rework, etc.	Current Activities, Immediate Needs	Planning. Development, Anticipation
Percentage	85%	10%	5%

This, in essence, is the "past trap" in which many of us find ourselves. But, just how do you get out of it? Well, if there were a simple answer, there would be no need for this book! We will, however, provide some guidance.

The first step toward the future is planning. We know we have said it before, but planning is essential. Without planning, you are just flirting with disaster. Besides, if you don't know where you are going, how will you know when you get there? So, determine what your needs are. How? By conducting a management audit. When you have evaluated the results, set your priorities and begin to implement effective corrective actions as outlined in Chapter 4 in which we described what to do after the audit using the following process (Figure 9.1).

We fully understand the difficulties with being trapped in the past. At the same time, we know it is possible to achieve positive results and to leave the past behind. It isn't painless, nor is the initial cost cheap, but the results are well worth the effort as the performance of companies that have achieved the Baldridge Award demonstrates. Now don't get us wrong. World class companies are not striving for perfection every step of the way. They are not looking for the "perfect solution" to any problem. While their performance expectations are high, they would tell you that waiting for the perfect solution leads to paralysis. Their emphasis is on improvement through the identification of actions that are achievable. These organizations have taken Deming's fifth principle to heart, and made it work for them.

This emphasis on the small, incremental change is important, but no less difficult to maintain. The basic practices may be described as follows:

1. **Measure.** The formula for continued improvement is to identify key process performance measures. The goal is not to "wallpaper" the operation with control charts, but to measure the important process performance characteristics. "Important" means the independent measures that are critical for the process to achieve the intended result. Usually, each process has four to six such measures which support the department measures. These, in turn, support the organizational goals and are those on which management decisions are based. While this description is an over-simplification, we believe it represents how these measures help the organization ensure system effectiveness.

2. **Monitor.** Observe the performance results. Numbers and process characteristics are recorded and analyzed to determine the effect they have on the process, the product, the system, and the customer. This is not a function that is, or should be, relegated to the inexperienced.

3. **Report.** The recording of information achieves little if it is not reported. Some reporting systems are very elaborate, but that is

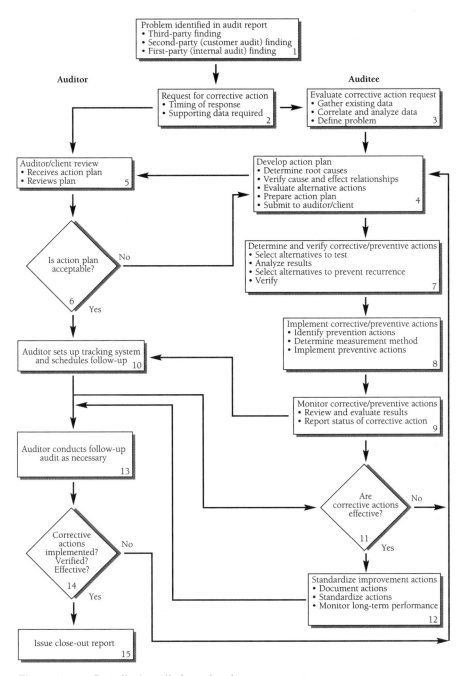

Figure 9.1. Detailed audit function improvement process.

not a requirement for effectiveness. One requirement is that if the data are not used to improve the process or system, don't report it, because it is not important. Yet, there are exceptions to this rule: for example, a customer may require that a specific characteristic be measured and reported. While the specified characteristic may have no immediate bearing on process improvement, such characteristics often have an impact on product design or performance.

4. **Summarize.** Reducing data to a concise and understandable form is necessary for long-term improvement. While the frequency of the reports varies by the nature of the data, most reporting systems are hierarchical (for example, daily, weekly, and monthly). Summarizing data in this way is beneficial for the identification of trends in performance so that long-term improvement may be achieved and maintained. When these performance trends include a comparison to the goal, organizations have an additional indicator to determine where the most improvement is needed. They also have the means to identify performance that is above expectations, and often evaluate the reasons for such performance. Addressing both the "surprises" and the "disappointments" provides an advantage that many organizations miss.

5. **Improve Performance.** Having noted the opportunities for improvement, each may then be addressed through a standardized corrective/preventive action plan. Most organizations employ a system similar to the one described in this book (see chapter 4). By applying the lessons learned from the unexpected improvements, you may enhance corrective/preventive actions by asking, "If we achieved improvement in that area, what prevents us from achieving the same result here?"

6. **Audit the System.** The quality system is evaluated to determine additional opportunities for improvement. The management of these organizations are not satisfied with the status quo as demonstrated by the normal reporting methods. They still desire and expect other opportunities for improved performance to be discovered through internal audits. Normally, these audits are more thorough than those of their customers because the auditors are not only well trained, they are also tenacious in their investigations.

For this formula to work effectively, it has to be management driven. Without the management focus, goals would not be set, the tools would not be provided, nor would the skills be developed to establish such an integrated approach.

Setting goals is important. Providing the resources to achieve them, such as providing the means to measure performance, and comparing the achieved level of performance to the established goals is equally important. Goals are neither positive nor negative and the purpose of the goals should be examined. If the purpose is long-term performance, and the resources to achieve them are provided, then goals should be considered positive and, therefore, beneficial to personnel and the organization. However, if the goals are only numbers to be achieved for their own sake with little consideration of the requirements to achieve them or the long-term benefit to the organization, then they become the program of the month with little added value. Such goals are negative because they are used for assessing personal performance without regard for organizational growth. Goals are used effectively by management to not only benefit the organization, but also to develop their personnel to perform better. What about personnel performance? Personnel performance assessment is very important, but should be done to the skill criteria necessary to improve the individual and organizational performance, not to blame some poor devil for being 0.2 below the specified output for the month. Goals are effective or not depending on their use and who assumes the responsibility for their achievement.

Such organizations maintain their high levels of performance because they have recognized the benefits of an effective internal audit program. Audits are well-planned and conducted by skilled, highly trained auditors. Audits are conducted to provide management with an audit of system effectiveness, not just to prepare for a customer visit or to ensure that the quota of audits has been completed prior to the return of the registrar. Organizations should be aware that some consultants and external auditors are locked irretrievably in the past, performing inspections rather than systems audits.

Ghosts from the Past

We continue to be haunted by ghosts from the past as the informal survey of our workshop participants demonstrates. In the introduction of each session of the workshops the authors conduct, participants are asked to state problems they have experienced achieving closure on audit corrective action. As we started to evaluate the information collected, the picture that was forming seemed to be overwhelmingly a lack of management support. There were a number of comments regarding management support and commitment, but there were also corrective action and timeliness issues. Obviously, these relate directly to management responsibility. Continuing to evaluate the information, however, we were surprised at the number of issues related to audit reports. When we completed the summary of the responses, we found they were grouped into seven categories which are listed below in order of their relative occurrence:

- Report Issues: 25.3%
- Management Support: 22.0%
- Root Cause Analysis: 12.1%
- Timeliness: 12.1%
- Closure Issues: 9.9%
- Corrective Action Effectiveness: 8.8%
- Corrective Action Training: 8.8%

If each of these were evaluated independently, we might conclude that everyone needs additional training, especially in corrective action. However, that is the easy, rather than the correct, conclusion. Consider these typical responses:

- Report contains insufficient detail
- Report does not match requirements
- Report does not present clear/concise description of the issue
- Report nonconformance not clearly explained
- Report not in Management Language ($s)
- Report not linked to Business Goals
- Report not stated clearly
- Report perceived too negatively
- Report provides detailed recommendations
- Report too personal
- Report traceability of details
- Report does not prove effectiveness
- Report identifies incorrect element
- Report incomplete
- Report lacking information

- Report not clear and not understood by management
- Report has only negative issues [Auditors]
- Report too detailed or not detailed enough

These responses indicate that either auditors are not reporting information correctly, or that they are not reporting the audit results in a manner that is meaningful to management. Of course, when we find that corrective actions are not implemented or that corrective actions are not timely, our conclusion, as auditors, is that management is not committed to the quality effort and will not, therefore, provide the necessary support to ensure corrective action is implemented and effective. However, claiming that the problem is a lack of management commitment is equivalent to a marketing manager complaining that there is no interest in cellular telephones when the product will only function in one limited area. The fact of the matter is that we have provided precious little motivation for management to initiate action in response to our reports. We should not be surprised, therefore, that "Management Support" immediately follows "Report Issues" in our groupings. As the cartoon character, Pogo, said, "We have met the enemy, and he is us."

If we recognize that our reports do not contain sufficient information, that they are not clearly written, and are incomplete, etc., then we should not expect management to be motivated to take action. The problem is neither management commitment nor corrective action.

**The problem is our failure to communicate the need
for change or improvement.**

Still, we should recognize that there may be a need for training in corrective action methods or improvement in corrective action. But, until we correct this fundamental communication or reporting issue, we *should not* expect management to take our audit reports seriously.

Compliance Audits

As surprising as it may seem, managers have also expressed their dissatisfaction with audit results. They lament the failure of audits to provide the continued benefits they have expected. We have observed that auditors continue to audit in the same manner, as by rote, using the same checklists, often asking the exact same information of the same people in every audit. Few have come to the realization that the audit program needs to mature *along with* the quality system. Neither the audit program nor the quality system should be static. Both should continue to evolve to support organizational needs. This transition, or evolution, of audit programs is not keeping pace with the organization because of the continued emphasis on compliance audits.

Now, don't misunderstand. There is nothing wrong with compliance audits. There is a need for them. When we implement a new system, we need to conduct compliance audits to ensure that the quality system requirements are being met. When we experience field problems, we may conduct a compliance audit to determine whether or not a system failure has occurred. However, we also should have recognized, by this time, that compliance audits have limitations.

Strictly speaking, compliance audits are little more than inspection. They are a comparison of "what is" against "what is required" by the applicable quality system standard. While this is a necessary activity in the implementation stage of a new system, their value declines rapidly as controls are effectively implemented. After a time, the issues reported have little, if any, impact on the improvement of the quality system. Instead, what is reported is a sporadic instance of a sloppy practice amid innumerable examples of proper, if not exemplary, practices. This is not to say that an isolated sloppy practice should be considered acceptable. Quite the contrary. But, it does not deserve the same attention that a serious breach of system controls does.

Fragmented Corrective Action

There was a time when product, process, and management audits were conducted on a regular, if not frequent, basis. These audits were abandoned in favor of compliance when customers began requiring certification at the height of the ISO craze. The primary reason was the resource requirements for the implementation process coupled with a preference to mimic the audit style of the registrar auditors. Unfortunately, their audit report style was also adopted to the detriment of the audit program as evidenced by our informal survey results. The survey responses have confirmed what our experience demonstrates:

Presenting lists of nonconformances is counterproductive.

The purpose of the audit report is to improve the organization's performance by identifying system improvement issues. Reports containing random common cause issues retard, rather than enhance, performance.

Any audit culminating in the presentation of a list of nonconformances to management is a failure.

When lists of nonconformances are transferred to individual and unrelated corrective action requests, the corrective action system is overloaded.

Consequently, the corrective action process is fragmented. Any improvement that would have resulted from the audit is defeated before corrective action begins because there are insufficient resources to address all of the individual issues. The solution, then, is to focus, rather than fragment, the corrective action process.

Focused Corrective Action

For organizations to realize enhanced performance as a result of audits, the recipients of the audit report need to:

- understand the system issues to be addressed
- recognize the benefit to the function, department, and/or organization
- have enough information to initiate effective corrective action

No matter how well an audit is conducted, these things will not be achieved if the audit team does not analyze the results from management's perspective. Nonconformances are only symptoms that may be either common cause or special cause events. However, management will not recognize the necessity for action unless provided the appropriate information.

Our failure to achieve focused corrective action is the result of our failure to communicate the need for change.

Focused corrective actions result from clearly stated system deficiencies, or findings, which are supported by evidence (grouped nonconformances). We must communicate the need for change when the audit is complete by analyzing the nonconformances to determine the system issues. By themselves, nonconformances are merely symptoms that have little impact on the system, but when they are grouped into related issues, they provide the means to identify the:

- system issue
- benefit to the function, department, and/or organization
- necessity for corrective action

Management's usual "so what" response is neutralized by the presentation of system concerns directly related to organizational performance issues.

The results of our informal survey indicate that audit reports provide management with very little information while auditors expect them to initiate great changes. If we are to motivate management to initiate change, we must first change the way we view systems audits, evaluate information, and present our audit results. We must, in fact, present the results of our audits from a management perspective. No matter what the quality system standard in use, that system is integrated into the organizational structure. Once the system is mature, or fully integrated, our audits should evolve into management audits to ensure continued effectiveness of the entire organization, of which the quality system is an integral element. Otherwise, we will continue to be haunted by ghosts from the past.

Is Registration Necessary?

Before any organization initiates the quality system certification process, the need for certification should be clearly defined. Several organizations with good quality management systems achieved certification to ISO 9000 or ISO 9000/QS 9000, but, after several years into the process, are questioning the benefit. The principal reason for their concern is their mistaken perception that they would gain market share by virtue of their certification. There are a few good reasons why external certification is necessary. Yet, when you think about it, there are really only two reasons for third-party registration.

Unbiased Quality System Validation

If there is one very good reason for an organization to have its quality system registered by an external body in this day of litigation, it would be product or service liability. External validation would be beneficial to a company by having an unbiased source answer the question: "Has the organization implemented a quality system which demonstrates that the customers' needs and requirements have been effectively addressed?"

Of course, the usual response is that an effective quality system does not guarantee good product. That is absolutely true. On the other hand, we have never seen a company with a shoddy quality system consistently deliver good product. The fact is that no quality system will guarantee perfect products. This "no guarantee" argument has been used from the beginning to avoid consideration of ISO and almost every other external certification, but the argument has never been developed beyond the basic objection itself. The fact is that it cannot be, because it is invalid as an argument. This is not the question to be asked because no company can guarantee 100 percent perfection.

The correct question is: "Has the organization implemented a quality system which demonstrates that the customers' needs and requirements have been effectively addressed?" Audits by customers, or second-party audits, cannot serve this purpose because they are not truly independent. Therefore, the lack of bias cannot be proven. Only independent, unbiased, third-party audits may best serve this purpose.

Customer Requirement

The other reason that an organization might seek third-party registration is when it is a requirement of the customer. Even when we are relatively successful, with a good reputation with our customers, we can hardly afford to ignore their requests. There are occasions when we may be able to discuss the customer's requirements, but even then we may not ignore them. The fact remains that when the customer decides what the quality system requirements will be, all of their subcontractors will be affected. While many of their subcontractors have worked hard to develop and maintain their quality system, others have not maintained the standards of performance that made them successful in the first place. Their customers have seen ISO 9000 registration as a means to bring all their subcontractors' performance up to the same level. So, they have made quality system registration a requirement for all subcontractors because a few have not properly developed their own quality systems. For that reason, when this situation presents itself, there are really only two types of subcontractors.

Companies with Unsatisfactory Quality Performance You may really believe that those subcontractors with unsatisfactory performance are just not really trying. After all, they must have done something right for them to have been so successful as long as they have been, and, therefore, they have just stopped trying to meet their customers' requirements. If you really believe that, then we can probably predict the industry you work in with a fair degree of accuracy. We have identified four categories into which organizations with unsatisfactory quality performance history may fall:

1. **Sheltered.** This is an organization whose quality system has been developed and maintained, but by their own standards of performance. Because they have made, and continue to make, improvements in their performance, they truly believe that they have implemented the best practices to be found anywhere. However, they have never ventured outside the confines of their own walls to realize that other companies have more advanced methods and are achieving far better results.

2. **Former Market Leader.** Once the best in their field, these companies believe that they really do understand the needs of their customers and that they are providing a product that exceeds their customers' requirements. Typical verification of their system's effectiveness is their question, "Why should we change when we have been satisfying our customers with these methods for the past 20 years?"

3. **Empowered (self-directed).** Empowerment is a wonderful concept, but there are organizations which have not bothered to understand either the concepts or their implications. Instead of empowerment, there is an abdication of responsibility because an assignment has been given to someone at a lower level in the organization. There is little preparation of personnel because they have been "empowered" (which means that if they need training, they will go and get it). All of which is well and good except for the fact that the primary element—communication—is left out of the entire process. As a result, the system is not monitored and it slowly deteriorates until disaster strikes.

4. **Rapid Growth (entrepreneurial).** Some companies are in the enviable position of being the sole manufacturer of a product, and everyone wants it. Because their business doubled "overnight" and each of the three years after, an ever increasing demand has been placed on a limited core group of skilled people. Even when they are able to locate people with the desired skills outside the company, these people do not know the product and must learn "on the fly" with no internal training. By the time they really begin to understand their customers' complaints, they are in serious trouble.

The organizations in each of these categories really do mean well. They all really want to satisfy their customers' requirements and, in many cases, believe they are doing so. Unfortunately for most, enlightenment is not a recognized need.

Companies with Exceptional Quality Performance. Good quality performance should have its rewards. And it does. As your customers will quickly tell you: "We are still doing business with you." Therefore, when a customer informs you that your company must be registered to this or that quality system standard, you will be expected to do so without argument. Although some companies have been "encouraged" to take the path of quality system certification, most with above average levels of performance have been proactive. They have incorporated the relevant ISO-like requirements into their quality management system before they became manadatory even though they continue to be the top performers for their customers. In spite of the fact that they are top performers, many of these companies have chosen to complete the registration process to demonstrate their continued quality commitment.

There are regulated industries where third-party registration may be a direct benefit. Exceptional quality performance history or not, they are expected to demonstrate a continued level of quality systems performance. These companies frequently find that the registration process, with periodic surveillance audits, helps them to identify concerns before problems occur.

Preparation for Third-Party Registration

Whatever your own particular situation, you will have a considerable amount of work to do. The ISO 9001 Quality Management System requirements have been incorporated into practically any industry you can name. Where ISO 9000 is not yet a requirement, it either has been or is being incorporated into the current quality standard of your customers. In order to prepare your quality system to meet the requirements of these new standards, there needs to be an organized process. If you are planning to do so, or are beginning the process, we would suggest that you consider the following.

Define the Purpose

Defining the purpose for your organization's pursuit of third party registration is important because it sets the stage for everything that is to follow. Even if it is a customer requirement, communicating the requirement to everyone in your organization is still an important and necessary consideration. Involve everyone in developing the timing plan for fulfilling the requirements of the standard.

Know the Requirements of the Standard

It goes without saying that to implement the standard, it must be understood. Frequently, there is too little training offered for those who must prepare system documentation. We have often recommended that those who are directly responsible for implementation attend training on the standard. What we mean is that staff personnel attend training on the requirements of the standard. However, that only provides the most basic understanding. To understand the relationship of one section to another, each person on the staff should be involved in an internal audit to the standard itself. Yes, it is a drastic measure, but you would not believe the number of times we have conducted auditor training courses only to hear the participants say: "I never really understood the requirements of this standard until now." It is a fact. You will not understand the nuances of any standard until you have prepared yourself to perform a thorough audit of a quality system to the requirements of that standard. During the course of the audit, you will develop a new understanding of the relationships which exist between one element to another. You will also develop a better understanding of the auditor's methods and how to respond during an audit.

Select and Train Internal Experts

There should be someone within the organization who fully understands the standard. This person will be invaluable in evaluating system documentation, helping to train and develop support personnel, and to keep everyone focused on the requirements of the standard. This person is most often the management representative in smaller organizations, but in larger organizations, there needs to be more than one person who is "fluent" in the requirements of the standard.

Other important roles for these individuals are conducting internal audits to the standard and to act as guides to the registrar's auditors during the registration audit. The need for the first is obvious, but the second is less so. Acting as a guide to the auditor, this individual can help to keep the auditor on track. He may also verify evidence found by the auditor, as well as indicate when the auditor has misinterpreted the evidence presented. In addition, this individual may be able to explain to the auditor the organization's reasons for answering a specific requirement in the manner it did *in the terms of the standard.*

Train Personnel to Be Audited

We have found that almost every organization will provide some form of training in the standard for management and staff personnel. Many will even develop an internal expert to assist the management representative. However, it is almost unheard of for an organization to instruct personnel in how to be audited. To us, this contradicts all the plans and preparations made. We have listed in chapter 4 some of the reasons why incorrect responses may be provided to an auditor. We have also observed that about one third of the nonconformities in an audit occur for those same reasons. Such occurrences may be reduced, if not eliminated, by providing instruction in how to respond to an auditor during an audit.

Plan for the Future

The fact that you have implemented a quality system that effectively addresses all the elements of the standard may well be demonstrated during the audit. But, if you are involved in continued improvement, what prevents you from discussing those plans with the auditor? Too often, we are left with the impression that the only improvement activities are centered around the activity of achieving registration, and that these activities will be at an end when registration is achieved. While such plans may not be a requirement of the standard, they will certainly demonstrate to the auditor that what has begun is to be a continuing process.

Select Your Registrar Carefully

If you are seeking third-party registration, you should determine the registrars that serve your industry. If your product is for an international market, you will also need to determine which registrars are accepted by your customers. When you have prepared a list of registrars, you should select your registrar with the same care you would an investment counselor. Take the time to visit several of the registrars at the top of your list. When you do, interview the management and some of the lead auditors to ensure that you have a good match for your needs.

You should also know that many registrars will want to persuade you that a preassessment, or, at the very least, a visit prior to the registration audit, is necessary to acquaint the auditors with your particular needs. In actual fact, we have not found any additional benefit from such visits, especially since few registrars allow those auditors conducting preassessments to participate in the registration audit.

This is not intended to be a definitive list of activities, but one that contains items of importance for your consideration as you develop your system. Initial planning and continuous communication throughout the process will help you achieve your goal.

Back to the Future

We have seen several good companies with effective audit programs that were not yet up to the standards of those in the "world-class" category. However, these companies have many similarities, not the least of which are open communication and the same positive "air" about them. By that, we mean that they recognize the realities of the manufacturing world, but have developed a culture that provides the type of open communication that is conducive to success. Their quality management system and their audits have matured to incorporate management audits rather than compliance audits. These companies have developed an effective method of reporting performance which aids them in their improvement efforts, but they have also prepared their personnel by demonstrating that process and system evaluation is good for the organization's development. In fact, their practice is reminiscent of this rhyme:[24]

Good, better, best

Never let it rest

Until the good becomes the better

And the better becomes the best.

Appendix A

Ideas for Improving the Auditing Product (Report)

A. Web Survey Response:
We asked people to share what they did to improve the effectiveness of the audit report (that is, provide a better product). The top responses were:

50%   issued new/modified reporting procedures

33%   set up an auditor feedback program

17%   provided training to improve the report formatting, style (language, terminology)

11%   provided additional communication equipment and resources

6%   upgraded pay and/or grade level for auditors

B. Other techniques and ideas shared by the survey participants for improving the report are:

- Audit customers asked for a common approach to reports and report formats. Our procedure was modified based on those customer requests. We also provide customer feedback forms after each audit.

- Computerized reporting already exists.

- Web access to the corrective action database is being developed. Formal Auditee feedback has been identified as an opportunity for improvement. Informal "customer" feedback has already been collected.

- Training is provided to veteran as well as newly trained internal auditors on how to format each audit report and how to address noncompliances when they are found. Detailed information is provided in the report to give the auditee all the information necessary to formulate an effective corrective action.

- Changed our procedures to state that the conclusion and summary of an audit can be combined.

- We are beginning to expand the audit process beyond compliance to the system. Increased process auditing and the initiation of "value-added" auditing are in their infancy.

- Our auditors have full time positions other than auditing. Any training or feedback for report writing would be conducted based on their reports submitted.

- We include a customer survey to get anonymous feedback from everyone that talks to an auditor. Results are tracked and communicated.

C. Other ideas:

- Discourage quick fixes to close out the audit report as fast as possible.

Appendix B

Ideas for Improving Post-Audit Activities (Follow-Up)

A. Web Survey Response:
We asked people to share what they did to improve the effectiveness of the post-audit activities and responsibilities. The top responses were:

50%   provide corrective action training for auditors and other stakeholders

44%   assign auditors as advisors to different areas but adhere to the no vested interest rule (that is, advisors cannot audit their own area)

44%   ensure experts and facilitators are made available to teams responsible for taking corrective action from the audit findings

38%   issued procedures/charts/guidelines to define post audit interfaces

38%   upgrade pay and/or grade levels for audit personnel

B. Other techniques and ideas shared by the survey participants for improving post-audit activities are:

- It is up to the area audited to evaluate the root cause(s) of the findings and form an action plan. These plans must be approved by the area manager and completed in a timely manner. Once this is accomplished, the auditor goes back to the unit and verifies that the nonconformance has been fixed, and that the fix is effective. Auditors are available to give advice, if requested.

- It was found that even though the auditee developed corrective actions, they were not properly documented or tracked for effectiveness. A corrective action committee was developed to review all submitted corrective actions which required documented root cause analysis and a process for tracking the effectiveness of the corrective action.

- I think our program is mature in this area. I may prepare a corrective action pamphlet for auditee managers and those who implement CA.

- While formally scheduled audits are taking place, informal walk-arounds are performed with supervisors, lead persons or engineering staff. This is done to recognize potential nonconformance and institute immediate corrections.

- We need to improve how we consider the effectiveness of corrective actions. A bit too subjective for right now.

C. Other ideas include:

- I have a one-on-one meeting to review the audit report with the manager of the area that was audited. I record that the meeting was held and the outcomes on a network document.

- Establish a criteria and grade the finding statements to stop poorly written or supported audit reports before passing on to auditee management.

- Establish a criteria for corrective action responses, publish it, expect it, enforce it.

- Require auditee to justify remedial action on corrective action response form. Explain why finding is an isolated incident and not a systemic problem.

Appendix C

Ideas for Auditing Customer Survey

A. Define the purpose of the survey
For example: To Provide feedback to the auditing service for continuous improvement and to achieve customer satisfaction.

B. Survey Design Considerations
Determine type of responses required:

- Answer questions: yes/no
- Response to statements: Strongly agree, Agree, Neutral, Disagree, Strongly Disagree
- Rate performance: 1 to 5, poor to excellent

Strategy:

- Determine what design basis would be most beneficial to the organization:
  - ~ Use process approach to link survey to planning-performing-reporting the service (see example question in this appendix).
  - ~ Use technical approach to link survey to auditor competency: technical expertise, auditing and communication skills, professionalism, and ethical conduct.

~ Use random approach to link survey to expressed/known needs and weaknesses.

- Keep the required responses to the minimum. In general, the fewer the required responses, the more likely you are to get the evaluation back.

- Avoid:

  ~ Asking what you should know. For example: Was the auditor properly trained?

  ~ Asking for suggestions you do not intend to use. For example: Should auditors be identified with a blue 'A' on their forehead? Should the auditor follow through and take corrective action on what they found?

  ~ Asking leading questions. For example: Did you receive the notification letter you were suppose to receive?

  ~ Asking serial biased questions. For example: Do you agree the President can influence the economy? Do you agree that the economy has been good over the last six years? Do you agree that the President has done a good job leading the economy?

- Determine who is supposed to complete the survey (your customers). For example: client, auditee representative, area manager, middle management, supervisor, each interviewee, auditee management team.

C. Timing: Timing may depend on organization culture and type of data you need to collect:

- After the closing meeting when the audit is still fresh on everyone's mind, ask auditee to complete the audit survey and send it in using a self-addressed stamped envelop. The survey should be independent of the auditor or audit team.

- Send the evaluation with the report and ask for it's return. Ask for the return of the evaluation form once the report is issued. Ask for feedback concerning the quality of the report.

D. Reporting results: The audit program management should analyze the results to identify individual, auditee and auditing service trends. Results should be used to foster positive trends and abate negative ones. Overall results should be linked to organization objectives and shared with management.

E. Example auditing service survey questions:

Plan

- Were you contacted by a member of the audit team to schedule the audit?
- Were your department needs and priorities considered when the audit was scheduled?
- Were you informed about the audit plan prior to the audit?
- Were you notified in advance that there was going to be an audit?*
- Where you notified of the audit: purpose, scope, start and end times, the performance standards used, team members?*

Performance

- Was the audit conducted on the date and time scheduled?
- Was an opening meeting held?* If not, was the opening meeting skipped at your request?
- Did the audit team explain the methods to be used to collect data during the audit?
- Did the auditors adequately answer your questions?
- Did the auditors stick to the interview schedule?
- Did the auditors stick to the agreed scope?
- Were the audited areas important to your organization?
- Were all the audit team members courteous and polite?
- Were the auditors courteous to interviewees?*
- Did the auditor(s) act professionally at all times?*
- Were the audit team members professional in their work and were they unbiased?
- Was a closing meeting held? Was it held immediately after the audit? If not, was the closing meeting skipped at your request?
- Did the auditor keep you informed of major findings during the audit?*
- Was there an exit meeting?*
- Did the auditor(s) leave a draft of the audit results?*
- Were you informed of when to expect the final report?*
- Were the stated audit objectives (purpose and scope) met?*

*Question taken from example survey form in text on page 152.

Report/Findings

- Were findings supported with evidence?
- Were the findings relevant to the organization?
- Were opportunities for improvement reported?
- Were positive practices or noteworthy achievements reported?
- Did the audit reveal information previously unknown to you?
- Was the final report provided in a timely manner?
- Did the report include both strengths and weaknesses?
- Was the audit report presented in a professional manner? [clean, unbiased, concise, clear, correct, complete]

Administration

- In your opinion, did the auditors possess the necessary knowledge for conducting audits and the standards being audited against?
- In your opinion, did the auditors have an understanding of the fundamental quality management principles needed to do the audit?
- In your opinion, was the audit team thorough? Were they able to probe deeply enough to gather meaningful information?
- Do you think the audits of your area should be done more or less frequently, and why?
- Do you plan to make changes to how work is conducted based on suggestions or opportunities for improvement shared by the audit team?
- Do you feel the results of the audit were understood? If not, why not?
- Please rate the overall value of the audit (not valuable, somewhat valuable, valuable, very valuable).
- Would you be willing to be audited by the same audit team again?*
- As a service, how would you rate the audit?*

Follow-up

- Were you informed of the expected follow-up actions to the audit report? [at the exit meeting and in the final report]
- If asked, were the auditors helpful in explaining what they observed as an aid to your follow-up actions?

*Question taken from example survey form in text on page 152.

Appendix D

Ideas for Linking Audit Program and Organization Objectives

A. Web survey response:
We asked people to share what steps they have taken to link audit program management with organizational objectives and culture. The top responses were:

44%   define audit program performance measures and report progress (for example, corrective action from audit benefits, corrective actions completed, repeat problems as a result of the same cause, cycle time reductions, customer satisfaction ratings, number of audit program complaints, etc.)

22%   initiate activities to promote the image of the audit group

22%   seek input and feedback from auditee organizations (survey forms, forums, group audit meetings)

22%   increase qualification criteria for auditors (up-grade caliber of auditor)

11%   develop a method to assess auditor performance (consistency)

B. Other techniques and ideas shared by the survey participants for improving the linkage between the audit program and organization objectives.

- Audit program management reports directly to the designated Quality System Management Representative. All reports are sent to the executive level, and are part of the quality systems review.

- Responsibility of corrective actions is assigned to the process owner. Audit results are part of the policy deployment metrics— the critical few metrics used to determine how well the facility's performing.

- Each organization unit is responsible for reviewing findings from their own areas at a defined interval. The quality assurance manager reports overall performance to a quality board, composed of senior managers, at least twice per year. Program performance measures have not been defined, nor have methods to assess auditor performance (other than timely completion).

- Systems are stale and inefficient. In process of revising, updating and implementing new, improved systems.

- The current quality manager is not an auditor and does not grasp the concept of improving the internal auditing process. To the QM this is just something that's required for ISO certification and as long as they remain certified with few noncompliances there is no need to change or improve the current program.

- Increased the qualification of auditors to state that they will become de-certified if they do not complete an audit in 18 months.

- Until recently, management had no set objectives for the audit program. Additionally, our training had always focused on compliance style auditing. Our attendance at the QA conference opened our eyes to the potential for further benefit to the company, with the value-added approach. We reviewed these ideas with our management and established goals for ourselves, which they approved.

- The quality system is at a very low maturity level despite being deployed for some time. The goal of management is to "fix" problems (fight fires).

- In addition to compliance, effectiveness of system is looked at, with feedback on possible design changes that could improve performance (quality, cost, productivity). Also looking at integrating audits of various management systems.

- Evaluation used and results tracked. New group is getting internal publicity. We need to link audit results to improved overall business results. The link is there.

Appendix E

Checklist for Auditing Quality Systems

Checklist[25] for ISO 10011-1, *Guidelines for auditing quality systems—Part 1: Auditing*

Clause Reference	Question
1.	**Scope**
	1. Has the organization developed specific procedures for implementing these auditing guidelines?
3.	**Definitions**
3.1.	**Quality audit**
	2. Is the audit carried out by staff not having direct responsibility for the areas being audited? (Note)
3.3.	**Auditor**
	3. Is the auditor authorized to perform the audit? (Note)
4.	**Audit objectives and responsibilities**
4.1.	**Audit objectives**
	4. Are audit objectives identified? —To determine conformity of the quality system with specific requirements

—To determine effectiveness of the implemented
system to meet specified quality objectives

—To provide the auditee with opportunity to improve
quality system; meet regulatory requirements

—To permit the listing of audited organization's quality
system with a registrar

5. Are the reasons for audit identified?

—To evaluate a potential supplier for contractual
purposes

—To determine if an organization's own quality system
meets requirements and is implemented

—To verify that the supplier's quality system continues
to meet their specific requirements and is
implemented

—To evaluate an organization's quality system against a
quality system standard

6. Has the audit resulted in transfer of responsibility from
operating staff to auditing organization? (Note)

7. Did the audit increase scope of responsibility of quality
function beyond those necessary to meet quality
objectives? (Note)

4.2. **Roles and responsibilities**

4.2.1. **Auditors**

4.2.1.1. **Audit team**

8. Has a lead auditor been appointed in overall charge?

9. Are experts, auditor trainees, observers identified as
part of the audit team and acceptable to the client,
auditee and lead auditor?

4.2.1.2. **Auditor's responsibilities**

10. Are auditor responsibilities defined as: complying with
audit requirements; communicating requirements;
planning and carrying out assigned responsibilities;
recording observations; reporting results; verifying
corrective action; controlling audit documents; and
cooperating with the lead auditor?

4.2.1.3. **Lead auditor's responsibilities**

11. Has the lead auditor taken responsibility for all phases
of the audit?

12. Does the lead auditor have management capabilities and experience?

13. Does the lead auditor have authority to make final decisions regarding the conduct of the audit and audit observations?

14. Do the lead auditor responsibilities include: assisting with the selection of other audit team members; preparing the audit plan; representing the audit team with the auditee's management; and submitting the audit report?

4.2.1.4.   **Independence of the auditor**

15. Are the auditors free from all bias and influences affecting objectivity?

16. Do persons and organizations involved with the audit respect and support the independence and integrity of the auditors?

4.2.1.5.   **Auditor's activities**

17. Have the lead auditor activities been defined to include:

   —Defining the requirements of each audit assignment, including auditor qualifications?
   —Complying with applicable auditing requirements and other directives?
   —Planning the audit, preparing working documents, and briefing the audit team?
   —Reviewing documentation on existing quality system activities?
   —Reporting critical nonconformances to auditee immediately?
   —Reporting any major obstacles encountered in audit?
   —Reporting the audit results clearly, conclusively, and without delay?

18. Do the auditor activities include:

   —Remaining within the audit scope?
   —Exercising objectivity?
   —Collecting evidence that is relevant and sufficient to permit conclusions?
   —Remaining alert to indications of evidence that can influence audit results and require more extensive auditing?

—Being able to answer questions and acting in an ethical manner at all times?

4.2.2. Client (person or organization requesting the audit)

19. Did the client determine the need for and the purpose of the audit and initiate the audit process?

20. Did the client determine the auditing organization?

21. Did the client receive the audit report?

22. Did the client determine what follow-up action is to be taken and inform the auditee of it?

4.2.3. Auditee

23. Has the auditee's management:

—Informed relevant employees about the scope and objectives of audit?

—Appointed responsible staff to accompany members of audit team?

—Provided resources for the audit team to ensure an effective and efficient audit process?

—Provided access to the facilities and materials requested by auditors?

—Cooperated with the auditors to permit audit objectives to be met?

—Determined and initiated corrective actions based on the audit report?

5. Auditing

5.1. Initiating the audit

5.1.1. Audit scope

24. Did the client identify the quality system elements, physical locations, and activities to be audited?

25. Was the auditee contacted when determining the scope of audit?

26. Does the scope and depth of the audit meet the client's specific information needs?

27. Did the client specify the standards or documents with which the auditee's quality system must comply?

28. Is sufficient objective evidence available to demonstrate the operation and effectiveness of auditee's quality system?

29. Are sufficient resources committed to the audit to meet scope and depth?

5.1.2. Audit frequency

30. Are audits scheduled based on specified or regulatory requirements and factors such as changes in management, organization, techniques, or technologies, or changes to the quality system?

31. Has the frequency of the internal audit schedule been determined? Note: It may be organized on a regular basis for management or business purposes.

5.1.3. Preliminary review of auditee's quality system description

32. Did the auditor conduct a preliminary review of the adequacy of the auditee's documented quality system for meeting the quality system requirements (such as the quality manual or equivalent)?

33. If not adequate, were all concerns resolved to the satisfaction of the client, auditor, and auditee (if applicable)?

34. Were all concerns resolved before continuing with the audit?

5.2. Preparing the audit

5.2.1. Audit plan

35. Has the audit plan been approved by the client and communicated to auditors and auditee?

36. Is the audit plan flexible to permit changes based on information gathered during the audit and to permit effective use of resources?

37. Does the plan include:

—Audit scope and objectives?
—Identification of individuals with direct responsibilities for objectives and scope?
—Identification of reference documents, audit team members, language of audit, and date and place where the audit is to be conducted?
—Identification of organizational units to be audited, with expected time and duration for each activity?

—The schedule of meetings to be held with auditee management?

—Confidentiality requirements, audit report distribution, and expected date of issue?

38. Have objections to provisions in audit plan by auditee been made known to the lead auditor?

39. Are all objections resolved before starting the audit?

40. Is the collecting of objective evidence compromised by the premature disclosure of specific audit plan details (data collection and sampling plans)?

5.2.2. Audit team assignments

41. Has each auditor been assigned specific system elements or functional departments to audit?

42. Were the auditors consulted by the lead auditor about the assignments prior to the audit?

5.2.3. Working documents

43. Are working documents required to facilitate the auditor investigations and to document and report results?

44. Do they include checklists for evaluating quality system elements, forms for reporting audit observations, and forms for documenting supporting evidence for conclusions reached by the auditors?

45. Do the working documents restrict additional audit activities or investigations as a result of information gathered during the audit?

46. Are the working documents suitably safeguarded to protect confidential or proprietary information?

5.3. Executing the audit

5.3.1. Opening meeting

47. Did the opening meeting include: introducing audit team members; reviewing scope and objectives of the audit; providing a summary of audit methods and procedures to be used to conduct the audit; establishing communication links between audit team and auditee; confirming resources and facilities needed by the audit team are available; confirming date and time for closing meeting; and clarifying any unclear details of the audit plan?

5.3.2.   **Examination**

5.3.2.1.   **Collecting evidence**

48. Is evidence collected through interviews, examination of documents, and observations of activities and conditions in the areas of concern?

49. Are significant clues suggesting nonconformances being noted even if not covered by checklists?

50. Are these clues being investigated?

51. Has information from interviews been tested from other independent sources like physical observations, measurements, and records?

52. Does the client approve and the auditee agree to changes in the audit plan if necessary to achieve audit objectives?

53. If the audit objectives are not attainable, is the lead auditor reporting the reasons to the client and auditee?

5.3.2.2.   **Audit observations (statements of fact supported by objective evidence)**

54. Are all audit observations documented?

55. Did the audit team review all observations to determine which observations will be reported as nonconformances?

56. Are all nonconformances documented in a clear, concise manner?

57. Are all nonconformances supported by evidence?

58. Are the specific requirements of the standard or other documents against which the audit was conducted identified for all nonconformances?

59. Did the lead auditor review all observations with the auditee management?

60. Has the auditee management acknowledged all observations of nonconformance?

5.3.3.   **Closing meeting with auditee**

61. Has a closing meeting been held with the auditee's senior management and concerned functions?

62. Were audit observations presented to senior management and the audit representatives in a manner such that they clearly understood the results of the audit?

63. Was the significance of the observations presented by the lead auditor?

64. Did the lead auditor present the audit team's conclusions on the effectiveness of the quality system to meet its quality objectives?

65. Were records of the closing meeting kept?

5.4.   Audit documents

5.4.1.   Audit report preparation

66. Did the lead auditor take responsibility for preparing the audit report and for its accuracy and completeness?

5.4.2.   Report content

67. Does the audit report faithfully reflect the tone and content of the audit as presented at the closing meeting?

68. Is the audit report dated and signed by the lead auditor?

69. Does the audit report contain

—The scope and objectives of the audit?
—Details of audit plan; identification of audit team members; auditee representative; audit dates; specific organization audited; and identification of reference documents against which the audit was conducted?
—Observations of nonconformances; audit team's judgment of auditee's compliance with applicable quality system standard or related document; and system's ability to achieve defined quality objectives?
—Audit report distribution list?

70. Is all communication between the closing meeting and issuing of report handled by the lead auditor?

5.4.3.   Report distribution

71. Has the report been sent to the client by the lead auditor?

72. Has the auditee's senior management been provided a copy of the audit report by the client?

73. Has the auditee been consulted for any additional distribution?

74. Are audit reports that contain confidential or proprietary information suitably safeguarded by the client and the auditing organization?

75. Is the report issued within the agreed-to time periods?

76. Are reasons for any audit report delays communicated to the client and auditee with a revised date established?

5.4.4.   Record retention

77. Are the audit documents retained in agreement with client, auditing organization, and auditee and in accordance with any regulatory requirements?

6.   Audit completion

There are no specific checklist questions for this section.

7.   Corrective action follow-up

78. Did the auditee take responsibility for determining and initiating corrective action to correct a nonconformance or to correct the cause of a nonconformance?

79. Has corrective action and follow-up audits been completed within the agreed-to time period?

80. Did the auditing organization keep the client informed of corrective action status and follow-up audits? (Note)

81. If there is a requirement for a follow-up report, has it been distributed in a similar manner as the original report? (Note)

Appendix F

Auditor Qualification Criteria Checklist

Checklist[26] for ISO 10011-2, *Guidelines for auditing quality systems—Part 2: Qualification criteria for quality system auditors*

Clause Reference	Question
4.	**Education**
1.	Has the auditor candidate completed at least secondary education?
2.	Has the candidate demonstrated competence in expressing concepts and ideas orally and in writing in the officially recognized language?
5.	**Training**
3.	Has the candidate been trained to competently carry out and manage audits?
4.	Has the candidate been trained in: knowledge and understanding of standards; assessment techniques of examining, questioning, evaluating, and reporting; and planning, organizing, communicating, and directing skills?

5. Has competence been demonstrated through oral or written examinations?

6. Experience

6. Does the candidate have a minimum of four years' full-time appropriate practical workplace experience?

7. Does the candidate have two years of experience in quality assurance activities?

8. Does the candidate have experience in the audit process described in ISO 10011-1?

9. Has the candidate participated in four audits, for a total of 20 days, including documentation review, audit activities, and audit reporting?

7. Personal attributes

10. Does the candidate possess personal attributes such as open-mindedness, maturity, sound judgment, analytical skills, and tenacity?

11. Does the candidate have the ability to perceive situations in a realistic way, to understand complex situations from a broad perspective, and to understand the role of units within the overall organization?

12. Can the auditor apply these attributes to:

—Obtain and assess objective evidence fairly; remain true to the audit without fear or favor?

—Evaluate constantly the effects of audit observation and personal interactions?

—Treat concerned personnel in a way that will best achieve the audit purpose; react with sensitivity to the national conventions of the country; perform the audit without distraction, commit full attention and support to the audit process; and react effectively in stressful situations?

—Arrive at acceptable conclusions based on audit observations?

—Remain true to a conclusion despite pressure to change not based on evidence?

8. **Management capabilities**

   13. Has the candidate demonstrated knowledge of and capability of using necessary management skills required in the execution of an audit as recommended in ISO 10011-1?

9. **Maintenance of competence**

   14. Is the auditor maintaining competency by having current knowledge of quality systems standards and requirements; auditing procedures and methods?

   15. Has the auditor participated in refresher training?

   16. Has the auditor performance been reviewed by an evaluation panel at least every three years?

   17. Does the auditor meet all the requirements of this part of ISO 10011?

   18. Does auditor review take into account information developed subsequent to the last review?

10. **Language**

   19. Do auditors participate in unsupported audits where they are not fluent in the language of audit?

11. **Selection of lead auditor**

   20. Did audit program management select the lead auditor for a specific audit?

   21. Did audit program management use the factors described in ISO 10011-3 to select the lead auditor?

   22. Did audit program management take into account the following criteria for selecting lead auditors?

      —Candidates acted as qualified auditors in at least three complete audits as recommended in ISO 10011-1

      —Candidates capably communicated orally and in writing in the agreed language of the audit

Annex A: Evaluating Auditor Candidates

Reference   Question

     A.1.   General

     A.2.   Evaluation panel

1. Has an evaluation panel been formed (established) for evaluating qualifications of auditor candidates?

2. Is the evaluation panel chaired by an individual currently active in managing audit operations?

3. Has the chairperson met the auditor qualifications recommended in ISO 10011-2?

4. Is the chairperson acceptable to a majority of other panel members and management?

5. Does the panel include representatives from other areas with current knowledge of the audit process?

6. Does the panel include clients and auditees who have been the subject of regular substantial audits?

6.A. For internal audits (first party); are panel members selected by management?

6.B. For customer audits (second party); are panel members selected by the customer unless otherwise agreed?

6.C. For independent third-party audits, are panel members selected by a board of management of a national certification scheme?

7. Does the panel contain at least two members?

8. Does the panel operate under defined rules and procedures?

9. Are rules and procedures designed to ensure the selection process is not arbitrary?

10. Are the criteria in agreement with ISO 10011-2 recommendations?

11. Is the operation of the panel free from conflict of interest?

A.3.   **Evaluations**

A.3.1.   **Education and training**

12. Is there evidence to show that the candidate has acquired the necessary knowledge and skills to carry out and manage audits?

13. Were the candidate skills evaluated by means of an examination by a national certification body or other means acceptable to the evaluation panel?

14. Did the panel make use of interviews with candidates, examinations, and candidates' written work to evaluate auditor candidates?

A.3.2.   **Experience**

15. Did the panel satisfy itself that the experience claimed by the candidate has actually been achieved?

16. Was the candidate experience gained within a reasonable time frame?

A.3.3.   **Personal attributes**

17. To assess personal attributes, did the panel use techniques such as:

—Interviews with candidates?
—Discussions with former employers, colleagues, and so on?
—Structured testing for appropriate characteristics?
—Role playing?
—Observations under actual audit conditions?

A.3.4.   **Management capabilities**

18. To assess management capabilities, did the panel use techniques such as:

—Interviews with candidates?
—Discussions with former employers, colleagues, and so on?
—Structured testing for appropriate characteristics?
—Role playing?
—Review records of training and related examinations?

A.3.5.   Maintenance of competence

19. Does the panel periodically review auditor performance, taking into account audit program management's assessment of performance?

20. Is any re-evaluation of auditor certification arising from these reviews carried out by the evaluation panel?

A.3.6.   Panel decisions

21. Does the panel only approve or disapprove the candidates?

22. Does review of performance result only in approval or disapproval?

23. Are all decisions recorded?

Appendix G

Audit Program Management Checklist

Checklist[27] for ISO 10011-3, *Guidelines for auditing quality systems—Part 3: Management of audit programs*

Clause
Reference   Question

     4.   **Managing an audit program**

   4.1.   **Organization**

       1.   Has overall management of the entire audit process been established by the organization with a need to carry out audits?

       2.   Is the audit management function independent of having direct responsibility for implementing the quality system being audited?

   4.2.   **Standards**

       3.   Has audit management identified the quality system standards they may audit against?

       4.   Has audit management developed capabilities to effectively audit against these standards?

4.3. Qualification of staff

4.3.1. Audit program management

5. Do the people responsible to carry out management of the audit program have practical knowledge of quality audit procedures and practices?

4.3.2. Auditors

6. Do the auditors employed by audit program management comply with recommendations in ISO 10011-2?

7. Have the auditors been approved by an evaluation panel that complies with ISO 10011-2?

4.4. Suitability of team members

8. Does audit program management ensure that the auditor skills are appropriate for each assignment by considering the following factors:

—Type of quality system standard against which the audit is conducted

—Type of service or product and it's associated regulatory requirements

—Need for professional qualifications or technical expertise

—Size and composition of the audit team

—Need for skill in managing the team

—Ability to make effective use of the skills of the various audit team members

—Personal skills needed to deal with a particular auditee

—The required language skills

—Absence of any real or perceived conflict of interest and other relevant factors

4.5. Monitoring and maintenance of auditor performance

4.5.1. Performance evaluations

9. Does audit program management continually evaluate the performance of the auditors?

10. Does audit program management use this information to improve auditor selection and performance and to identify unsuitable performance?

11. Does audit program management make this information available to evaluation panels?

4.5.2.   Consistency of auditors

12. Do audits conducted by different auditors arrive at similar conclusions when the same operation is audited?

13. Have methods been established by audit program management to achieve consistency?

14. Do these methods include:

   —Auditor training workshops, auditor performance comparisons?
   —Reviews of audit reports, performance appraisals, and rotation of auditors?

4.5.3.   Training

15. Does audit program management regularly assess the training needs of auditors?

16. Are appropriate actions taken to maintain and improve audit skills?

4.6.   Operational factors

4.6.1.   General

17. Are procedures established by audit program management to ensure the audit staff can operate in a consistent manner and are adequately supported?

4.6.2.   Commitment of resources

18. Are procedures established to ensure adequate resources are available to accomplish audit objectives?

4.6.3.   Audit program planning and scheduling

19. Are procedures established for planning and scheduling the audit program?

4.6.4.   Audit reporting

20. Are audit reports formalized to the extent practical?

4.6.5.   Corrective action follow-up

21. Are procedures established to control corrective action follow-up if audit program management is requested to do so?

4.6.6. Confidentiality

22. Are procedures established by audit program management to safeguard the confidentiality of an audit or auditor information?

4.7. Joint audits

23. Has agreement been reached on the specific responsibilities of each organization involved in a joint audit, in regard to lead auditor authority, interfaces with the auditee, methods of operation, and distribution of audit reports?

24. Has this agreement been reached before the audit begins?

4.8. Audit program improvement

25. Has audit program management established a method of continuously improving the audit program through audit customer feedback and recommendations from all parties?

5. Code of ethics

26. Has audit program management considered the need for a code of ethics in the operation and management of the audit program?

Appendix H

Corrective and Preventive Action Procedure

Distribution List

All quality manual holders

1. **Purpose**

   To establish controls for taking corrective and preventive action on identified problems or negative trends identified through analysis of quality records.

2. **Scope**

   This procedure applies to internal or external concerns relating to quality, reliability, safety, or performance of any product or service offered by the company. Specifically, the procedure covers action taken from nonconforming product (including purchased product), customer complaints, audit findings, and negative trends identified from analysis of quality records (to include complaints, findings, nonconforming product reports, work processes, concessions, and service reports).

3. **Responsibilities**

   All employees have the responsibility to initiate corrective/preventive action requests for known problems.

The quality assurance manager is responsible for establishing, implementing, maintaining, and the ongoing effectiveness of the corrective/preventive action program.

4. **Reference Documents**

   Purchasing Procedure 7.401

   Control of Nonconforming Product Procedure 8.301

   Internal Quality Audit Procedure 8.201

   CAR form F8.508

5. **Definitions**

   Remedial action: an action taken to alleviate the symptoms of existing nonconformities or any other undesirable situation.

   Corrective action: an action taken to eliminate the cause(s) of existing nonconformities (problems) or any other undesirable situation in order to prevent recurrence.

   Preventive action: an action taken to eliminate the cause(s) of potential nonconformities (problems) in order to prevent occurrence.

6. **Procedure**

   6.1 The person who detected the problem (originator) should initiate a corrective/preventive action request (CAR) form. Problem sources include supplier nonconformance, internal nonconforming product, customer complaints, audit findings, and the results of analysis of quality records. The CAR form should be forwarded to the quality assurance manager.

   6.2 The quality assurance manager logs and reviews the CAR to assess the magnitude (importance of the problem). The quality assurance manager then assigns an employee to resolve the problem and requests a corrective action plan within a certain time frame (depending on the complexity and importance of the problem). The CAR is forwarded to the employee assigned the corrective action. For audit findings, the CARs are automatically assigned to the area that was audited.

   6.3 The person assigned evaluates the corrective action request to determine if this is an isolated occurrence or a system problem. It may be necessary to restate the problem as a system concern or to relate it to customer requirements.

6.4 The person assigned the CAR investigates by collecting data to determine the cause(s) of the problem (nonconformance, complaint). The person assigned may determine the causes or the person may decide other individuals need to be involved (form a corrective action team to be disbanded when the corrective action is implemented). The results of the investigation must be recorded.

6.5 The person assigned the CAR determines the corrective/preventive action (or alternative solutions) needed to eliminate the root cause (underlying cause) of the problem and the measure(s) to be used to verify its effectiveness (if it fixed the problem). The corrective action plan must be recorded and returned to the originator (lead auditor, if from an audit finding).

Note: If an extension is needed, a memo must be submitted to the originator of the corrective action and the quality assurance manager stating the additional time needed and reason for the extension. The quality assurance manager files the memo with the open CAR.

6.6 The originator accepts or rejects the planned corrective action and forwards the CAR form to the quality assurance manager. The quality assurance manager records the status of the CAR and forwards to the person assigned the corrective action.

6.7 The person assigned the corrective action either moves forward with implementation of the plan or returns to step 6.4 if the proposed corrective action has been rejected.

6.8 Unresolved corrective actions must be brought to the attention of the quality assurance manager. The corrective action plan will be finalized at a meeting with the quality assurance manager, originator, and the person assigned the corrective action.

6.9 The implementation of the corrective action is turned over to the appropriate individuals or department who can take action. The quality assurance manager should be notified of the planned implementation date. Implementation should

CORRECTIVE ACTION REQUEST

Date:	CAR number:

Auditee/Area:

Audit number:

Finding/Problem:

Contact	Auditor/Originator
Signature: _____	Signature: _____
Title: _____	Title: _____

Remedial
Action:

Root
Cause:

Action
Plan:

Corrective Start Complete	
Action	Auditor
Plan Dates:	Acceptance: Date:

Corrective/
Preventive
Action
Taken:

Signature: _____   Date:

Corrective   Corrective
Action   Action
Approved [   ] Disapproved [   ]   Auditor: _____

Follow-Up Audit Date: Signature: _____

Close-Out Date: Signature: _____

Example of simple Corrective Action Form

include permanent changes to documents, equipment, and processes.

6.10 After the implementation date, the corrective action should be verified either through an audit or analysis of data (the measures) or personal observation. Verification will result in closure of the CAR.

6.11 The quality assurance manager is responsible for ensuring that corrective action process is monitored. Monitoring should include review of the status of open CARs and overall evaluation of the effectiveness of corrective action program. Effectiveness measures could include whether root causes are being identified, whether the company is benefiting, whether resolution dates are being achieved.

The quality assurance manager must report the status of CARs and effectiveness of the corrective action program to the management review committee at each meeting.

Notes

1. ISO 10011-1, *Guidelines for auditing quality systems—Part 1: Auditing* (Geneva, Switzerland: International Organization for Standardization, 1993), clause 6.0.

2. Survey 903A: Improving audit program effectiveness. Web page www.JP-Russell.com, March 1999 through Sept 1999, J.P. Russell and Associates, Gulf Breeze, FL, complete results posted on web page.

3. ISO 10011-1, clause 3.8.

4. Dennis Arter, *Quality Audits for Improved Performance,* 2nd ed. (Milwaukee: ASQC Quality Press, 1994), 56.

5. W. Edwards Deming, *Out of the Crisis* (Cambridge, MA: MIT Center for Advanced Engineering Study, 1982), 88.

6. Walter A. Shewhart, *Statistical Methods from the Viewpoint of Quality Control* (New York: Dover Publications, 1938).

7. Brian L. Joiner, *Fourth Generation Management: The New Business Consciousness* (New York: McGraw-Hill, 1994), 44.

8. This example provided by Tom Taormina from Productivity Resources, Bellville, TX 77418, author of *Virtual Leadership and the ISO 9000 Imperative*. Reprinted with permission.

9. ISO/DIS 9001, *Quality management systems—Requirements* (Geneva, Switzerland: International Organization for Standardization, 1999), clause 8.5.2.

10. *Statement of Internal Auditing Standards Glossary* (Altamonte Springs, FL: Institute of Internal Auditors), 24 May 1995 and standards 410.01 and 520.04.2.

11. ISO 10011-1, clause 7.0.

12. Ibid., clause 4.3.

13. Ibid., clause 4.1.

14. ISO 9001, clause 4.1.

15. Ibid., clause 5.6.1.

16. Ibid., clause 8.22.

17. Ibid., clause 8.4.

18. The *Quality Audit Handbook,* 2nd Ed, ASQ QAD Division, 2000 Quality Press. Milwaukee, ASQ Quality Press.

19. Stephen R. Covey, *The 7 Habits of Highly Effective People* (New York: Simon & Schuster, 1989).

20. *Statement of Internal Auditing Standards Glossary.*

21. *ACSI Update* (Milwaukee: ASQC Quality Press, 1990).

22. J. P. Russell, *The Quality Master Plan* (Milwaukee: ASQC Quality Press, 1990).

23. ISO 10011-3, *Guidelines for auditing quality systems—Part 3: Management of audit programmes* (Geneva, Switzerland: International Organization for Standardization, 1991), clause 4.8.

24. Lewis D. Eigen and Jonathan P. Siegel, *Quotations* (New York: AMACOM), 378.

25. J. P. Russell, *ISO 123 Data Disk* (Allentown, Pa.: Columbia Quality, 1994).

26. Ibid.

27. Ibid.

Glossary

Definitions in this glossary have been referenced to known source as appropriate. Where no source for a definition is given, either ordinary American English usage is intended or it is a definition originating from this work.

Note: Some definitions have been updated to include the revised definitions contained in the ISO/DIS 9000:2000 which replaces ISO 8402. All reference to ISO/DIS 9000:2000, Quality Management Systems—Fundamentals and Vocabulary, Geneva, Switzerland, International Organization for Standardization, will be indicated as ISO 9000.

ASQ: American Society for Quality. ASQ is located at 611 East Wisconsin Avenue, P. O. Box 3005, Milwaukee, WI 53201-3005, telephone 800-248-1946, fax 414-272-1734.www.asq.org

Assessment: An estimate or determination of the significance, importance, or value of something. [ASQ Certification, CQA Booklet, Milwaukee, 1995.]

Audit (1): A planned, independent, and documented assessment to determine whether agreed-upon requirements are being met.

Audit (2): A formal examination of an organization's or individual's accounts or financial situation. [*Webster's Collegiate Dictionary*, Houghton Mifflin Co., 1990 edition.]

Audit (3): A systematic, independent, and documented process for obtaining evidence and evaluating it objectively to determine the extent to which audit criteria are fulfilled. [ISO 9000.]

Audit report: A signed, written document which presents the purpose, scope and results of the audit (partial definition). [Internal Auditing Standards Board, Institute of Internal Auditors, Glossary, Altamonte Springs, Fla., 1995 draft.]

Auditee: Organization being audited. [ISO 9000] Includes any unit or activity within an organization that is audited. [Internal Auditing Standards Board, Institute of Internal Auditors, Glossary.]

Auditor: A person who is qualified to assist a lead auditor in performing a portion of an audit assignment. Also known as an audit team member. Also authorized to perform all or part of an audit. [Arter, *Quality Audits for Improved Performance.*]

Auditor (quality): A person qualified to conduct quality audits. [ISO 9000.]

Bad fact: An undesirable occurrence of an event which is contrary to stated or accepted levels of performance. May also be known as *nonconformity.*

Benchmark: A point of reference from which measurements and conclusions can be made. Organizations can benchmark to compare their operation to competition (competitive benchmarking) and/or to compare their quality systems to generally recognized quality management standards and criteria. [J. P. Russell, *Quality Management Benchmark Assessment,* 2nd ed.] ASQC Quality Press, Milwaukee, 1995.

Benchmarking: An improvement process in which a company measures its performance against that of best-in-class companies, determines how those companies achieved their performance levels, and uses the information to improve its own performance. The subjects that can be benchmarked include strategies, operations, processes, and procedures. [Compiled by Karen Bemowski for *Quality Progress,* February 1992.]

Capability: Also called process capability, a statistical measure of the inherent process variability for a given characteristic. For example, the standard deviation of a multiple of the standard deviation. [Ishikawa *Guide to Quality Control,* New York: Kraus International Publications, 1982, p. 145.]

Capability (process) **Index, Cp** or **Cpk:** A statistical measure used to describe the capability of a process to produce a product (output) within specification (tolerance limits). Each index is the value of the tolerance (specification range) for the characteristic divided by the process capability. The index is a measure that indicated high or low process variability. Note: Where k is a constant number of subgroups of a given size. [Ishikawa, *Guide to Quality Control.*]

Capable: A process with a stable pattern of behavior within the upper and lower specification limit.

Common causes: Causes of variation that are inherent in a process over time. They affect every outcome of the process and everyone working in the process. Note: Refer to *special causes* for more information. [Compiled by Karen Bemowski for *Quality Progress.*]

Client: A person or organization requesting the audit.

Conformance: An affirmative indication or judgment that a product or service has met the requirements of the relevant specification, contract, or regulation. [Compiled by Karen Bemowski for *Quality Progress.*]

Conformity: Fulfillment of a requirement. [ISO 9000.]

Continuous improvement: The ongoing improvement of products, services, or processes through incremental and breakthrough improvements. [Compiled by Karen Bemowski for *Quality Progress.*]

Control chart: A graphical method for evaluating whether a process is or is not in a "state of statistical control." [Ishikawa, *Guide to Quality Control.*]

Control limits: Limits on a control chart that are used as criteria for signaling the need for action, or for judging whether a set of data does or does not represent a "state of statistical control." [Ishikawa, *Guide to Quality Control.*]

Corrective action (1): Action taken to eliminate the cause of a detected nonconformity or other undesirable situation in order to prevent recurrence. [ISO 9000.]

Corrective action (2): The implementation of solutions resulting in the reduction or elimination of an identified problem. [Compiled by Karen Bemowski for *Quality Progress.*]

Quality costs (COQ): The price of doing it wrong (costs of not conforming to requirements) and the price of inspecting and checking (cost of procedures, appraisals, and compliance) added together.

Customer: The recipient of a product (service) provided by the supplier. [ISO 8402.] *External customer* is a person or organization who receives a product, a service, or information but is not part of the organization supplying it. [Compiled by Bemowski for Quality Progress.] *Internal customer* is the recipient (person or department) of another person's or department's output (product, service, or information) within an organization. [Compiled by Karen Bemowski for *Quality Progress.*]

Data: Information, contained in records, that results from the operation of a process or system.

Document: An original or official paper relied on as the basis, proof, or support of something. A writing conveying information. [*Webster's Ninth Collegiate Dictionary,* 1990.]

Effective control: Is present when management directs systems in such a manner as to provide reasonable assurance that the organization's objectives and goals will be achieved. [Internal Auditing Standards Board, Institute of Internal Auditors, Glossary.]

Effective performance: Accomplishes objectives and goals in an accurate and timely fashion with minimal use of resources. [Internal Auditing Standards Board, Institute of Internal Auditors, Glossary.]

Fact: The state of things as they are. [*Webster's New World Dictionary.*]

Feedback: Information provided for evaluation and improvement.

Finding (1): A conclusion or importance based on observation(s). [ASQ Certification, CQA Booklet.]

Finding (2): An audit conclusion based on objective evidence stating a system weakness related to organizational goals.

Finding (3): An audit conclusion that identifies a condition that has a significant adverse effect on the quality of the goods or services produced. An audit finding contains both cause and effect and is normally accompanied by several specific examples of the observed condition. [Arter, *Quality Audits for Improved Performance.* 1994, 2nd Ed, Quality Press, Milwaukee.]

Flowchart: A graphical representation of the steps in a process. Flowcharts are drawn to better understand processes. The flowchart is one of the seven tools of quality.

Failure Mode and Effects Analysis (FMEA): An FMEA can be described as a systematized group of activities intended to: (1) recognize and evaluate the potential failure modes and causes associated with the designing and manufacturing of a product, (2) identify actions which could eliminate or reduce the chance of the potential failure occurring, and (3) document the process. It is complementary to the prime design process of defining positively what a design must do to satisfy the customer. [*Potential Failure Mode and Effect Analysis,* Ford Motor Company, 1988, p. 1.]

Follow-up: Conducted by internal auditors, is defined as a process by which auditors determine the adequacy, effectiveness, and timeliness of actions taken by management on reported audit findings. Such findings also include relevant findings made by external auditors and others. [Internal Auditing Standards Board, Institute of Internal Auditors, Glossary.]

Follow-up audit: An audit whose purpose and scope are limited to verifying that corrective action has been accomplished as scheduled and to determine that the action prevented recurrence effectively. [ASQ Certification, CQA Booklet.]

Goals: Specific objectives of specific systems and may be otherwise referred to as operating or program objectives or goals, operating standards, performance levels, targets, or expected results. [Internal Auditing Standards Board, Institute of Internal Auditors, Glossary.]

In control: A process in which the statistical measure(s) being evaluated are in a "state of statistical control." [Compiled by Bemowski for Quality Progress.] The term process may represent (a) the manufacture of physical and tangible products, (b) the output of services, (c) the collection of measurements, and (d) other activities such as paperwork.

Independence: Freedom from bias and external influences. [ASQ Certification, CQA Booklet.]

Independent: Not directly responsible for the quality, cost, and/or production of goods or services being examined. [Arter, *Quality Audits for Improved Performance.* 1994, 2nd Ed, Quality Press, Milwaukee]

ISO 9000 Series Standards: A set of quality management system standards issued by the International Organization for Standardization (a worldwide federation) and used by companies that produce products and services. The American version of the ISO 9000 Standards are the ANSI/ISO/ASQC Q9000 Series Standards.

Lead auditor: An individual qualified to plan, organize, and direct audits, report audit findings, and evaluate corrective actions.

Lead team: A team that sponsors another team whose mission is essential to its own success.

Malcolm Baldrige National Quality Award Guidelines: Examination criteria designed for the evaluation of the strengths and areas for improvement in the organization's quality system and of quality results. Guidelines are available from ASQ or National Institute of Standards and Technology.

Management: Includes anyone in an organization with responsibilities for setting and/or achieving objectives. [Internal Auditing Standards Board, Institute of Internal Auditors, Glossary.]

Monitoring: Encompasses supervising, observing, and testing activities and appropriately reporting to responsible individuals. Monitoring provides an ongoing verification of progress toward achievement of objectives and goals. [Internal Auditing Standards Board, Institute of Internal Auditors, Glossary.]

Objectives: The broadest statement of what the organization chooses to accomplish. [Internal Auditing Standards Board, Institute of Internal Auditors, Glossary.]

Nonconformity: The nonfulfillment of specified requirements.

Operation: A single step in a process.

Out-of-control process: A process in which the statistical measure being evaluated is not in a state of statistical control (that is, the variations among the observed sampling results can be attributed to a constant system of chance causes). [Compiled by Karen Bemowski for *Quality Progress*.]

Plan-Do-Check-Act (PDCA) cycle: A four-step process for quality improvement. In the first step (Plan), a plan to affect improvement is developed. In the second step (Do), the plan is carried out, preferably on a small scale. In the third step (Check), the effects of the plan are observed. In the last step (Act), the results are studied to determine what was learned and what can be predicted. [Compiled by Karen Bemowski for *Quality Progress*.]

Performance standard: Expectation of how a job or task should be done according to requirements and specifications.

Preventive action: Action taken to eliminate the cause of a potential nonconformity or other potentially undesirable situation in order to prevent occurrence. [ISO 9000.]

Prevention: The improvement achieved through detailed analysis of a process in order to determine potential concerns and eliminate the occurrence of such concerns in a product, process, or service.

Prevention versus detection: A phrase used to contrast two types of quality activities. Prevention refers to those activities designed to prevent nonconformances in products and services. Detection refers to those activities designed to detect nonconformities already in products or services. [Compiled by Karen Bemowski for *Quality Progress*.]

Process: A set or series of conditions, operations, or steps, working together to produce a desired result.

Quality (1): Ability of a set of inherent characteristics of a product, system, or process to fulfill requirements of customers and other interested parties. [ISO 9000.]

Quality (2): A subjective term for which each person has his or her own definition. In technical usage, quality can have two meanings: (1) the characteristics of a product or service that bear on its ability to satisfy stated or implied needs and (2) a product or service free of deficiencies. [Compiled by Karen Bemowski for *Quality Progress*.]

Quality (3): For the customer, quality is getting what you were expecting; for the supplier, quality is getting it right the first time.

Quality assurance: Part of quality management, focused on providing confidence that quality requirements are fulfilled. [ISO 9000.]

Quality control: Part of quality management, focused on fulfilling quality requirements. [ISO 9000.]

Quality management: Coordinated activities to direct and control an organization with regard to quality. [ISO 9000.]

Quality manual (1): A document that states the quality policy, system, and practices of an organization.

Quality manual (2): A document specifying the quality management system of an organization. [ISO 9000.]

Quality management system: System to establish a quality policy and quality objectives and to achieve those objectives. [ISO 9000.]

Quality policy: Overall intentions and direction of an organization related to quality as formally expressed by top management. [ISO 9000.]

Quality waiver: A document approving the shipment or delivery of products or services that do not meet one or more specification (requirement) properties.

Record: Document stating results achieved or providing evidence of activities performed. [ISO 9000.]

Record (2): A written description of an activity that has been accomplished. [Arter, *Quality Audits for Improved Performance.* 1994, 2nd Ed, Quality Press, Milwaukee]

Recommendations: Actions the auditor believes necessary to correct existing conditions or improve operations. [Internal Auditing Standards Board, Institute of Internal Auditors, Glossary.]

Requirement: A need or expectation that is stated, customarily implied or obligatory. [ISO 9000.]

Risk: The probability that an event or action may adversely affect the organization or activity (partial definition used). [Internal Auditing Standards Board, Institute of Internal Auditors, Glossary.]

Root cause: A fundamental deficiency that results in a nonconformance and must be corrected to prevent recurrence of the same or similar nonconformance. [ASQC, *Certified Quality Auditor Booklet,* 1995.] Note: This definition is weak because it presupposes a nonconformance and it is not clear that the definition includes root causes of potential problems.

Sample: One of more units of product (or a quantity of material) drawn from a specific lot or process for purposes of inspection to provide information that may be used as a basis for making a decision concerning acceptance of that lot or process. [Dr. Kaoru Ishikawa, *Guide to Quality Control* 1982 Kraus International Publications, White Plains, NY.]

Sample size: Number of units in a sample.

Special causes: Causes of variation that arise because of special circumstances. They are not an inherent part of the process. Special causes are also referred to as assignable causes. [Compiled by Karen Bemowski for *Quality Progress.*]

Statistical quality control (SQC): The application of statistics for the control of a process or system.

Statistical control: A process is considered to be in a "state of statistical control" if the variations among the observed sampling results can be attributed to a constant system of chance causes.

Supplier: A company or individual who provides input to processes (jobs), whether from inside the company or external to it. In quality improvement, the customer/supplier relationship becomes an interactive relationship that calls for sharing requirements and expectations.

System: A collection of processes supported by an infrastructure to manage and coordinate its function.

Verification (1): The act of reviewing, inspecting, testing, checking, auditing, or otherwise establishing and documenting whether items, processes, services, or documents conform to specified requirements. [*Chemical,* p. 107].

Verification (2): Confirmation and provision of objective evidence that requirements for a specific intended use or application have been fulfilled. [ISO 9000:2000.]

Suggested Reading

Adams, James L. *Conceptual Blockbusting: A Guide to Better Ideas.* 2nd. ed. New York: W. W. Norton, 1979.

Arter, Dennis R. *Quality Audits for Improved Performance,* 2nd ed. Milwaukee: ASQC Quality Press, 1994.

Barker, Joel Arthur. *Future Edge: Discovering the New Paradigms of Success.* New York: William Morrow and Company, 1992.

Barry, Thomas J. *Excellence Is a Habit: How to Avoid Quality Burnout.* Milwaukee: ASQC Quality Press, 1994.

Boyett, Joseph H., and Henry P. Conn. *Workplace 2000: The Revolution Reshaping American Business.* New York: Dutton, 1991.

Boyles, Jerry, and Joshua Hammond. *Beyond Quality: How 50 Winning Companies Use Continuous Improvement.* New York: Putnam, 1991.

Byham, William C. *Zapp!: The Lightening of Empowerment.* New York: Harmony Books, 1988.

Cartin, Thomas J. *Principles & Practices of Organizational Performance Excellence.* Milwaukee: ASQ Quality Press, 1999.

Cohen, Allan R., and David L. Bradford. *Influence Without Authority.* New York: John Wiley & Sons, 1990.

Deming, W. Edwards. *Out of the Crisis.* Cambridge, MS: MIT Center for Advanced Engineering Study, 1986.

Harrington, H. James. *The Improvement Process: How America's Leading Companies Improve Quality.* New York: McGraw-Hill, 1987.

Joiner, Brian L. *Fourth Generation Management: The New Business Consciousness.* New York: McGraw-Hill, 1994.

Juran, J. M. *Juran on Planning for Quality.* New York: Free Press, 1988.

Kotter, John P. *A Force for Change: How Leadership Differs from Management.* New York: Free Press, 1990.

Lumsdaine, Edward and Monica Lumsdaine. *Creative Problem Solving: Workshop Manual for Managers and Engineers.* Toledo, OH: 1989.

Manske, Fred A., Jr. *Secrets of Effective Leadership: A Practical Guide to Success.* 2nd. ed. Columbia, TN: Leadership Education and Development, 1990.

Oakley, Ed, and Doug Krug. *Enlightened Leadership: Getting to the Heart of Change.* New York: Simon & Schuster, 1991.

Roberts, Harry V., and Bernard F. Sergesketter. *Quality Is Personal: A Foundation for Total Quality Management.* New York: Free Press, 1993.

Russell, J. P. *The Quality Master Plan.* Milwaukee: ASQC Quality Press, 1990.

Sayle, Allan J. *Management Audits.* 3rd ed. Brighton, MI: Allan Sayle Associates, 1997.

Scherkenbach, William W. *The Deming Route to Quality and Productivity: Road Maps and Roadblocks.* Milwaukee: ASQC Quality Press, 1988.

Woolf, Bob. *Friendly Persuasion: How to Negotiate and Win.* New York: Berkley Books, 1990.

Index